ENJOY
Black & Mild®
FILTER TIP CIGARS
── SHORT. SMOOTH. ──

HORNITOS®

TEQUILA REPOSADO RESTED

AGAVE

100% PURO DE AGAVE
· 40% ALC/VOL · 750 mL ·

HORNITOS®

TEQUILA PLATA UNAGED

100%

AGAVE

100% PURO DE AGAVE
· 40% ALC/VOL · 750 mL ·

HORNITOS®

100%

NATURAL? YES.
DELICIOUS? YES.
OSCAR MAYER?
ABSOLUTELY!

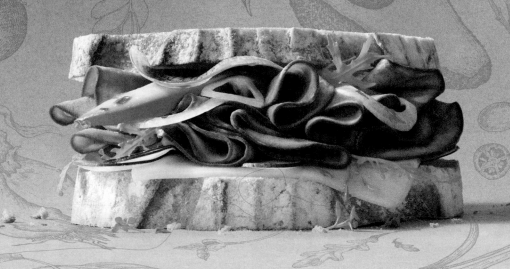

NO ARTIFICIAL INGREDIENTS. NO ANTIBIOTICS. EVER.

Contents

ISSUE 1331
'ALL THE NEWS THAT FITS'

"Some of the things he does scare the hell out of me."

Brad Shultz
The Cage the Elephant guitarist talking about his brother, Cage singer Matt Shultz

20

PHOTOGRAPH BY **Sacha Lecca**

Contents

24

PHOTOGRAPH BY **Griffin Lotz**

Technology that brings people together in an SUV that stands apart.

Introducing the new 2020 Mercedes-Benz GLC. The more time you spend in it, the more it gets to know you and your passenger's preferences. Its intelligent voice controlled Mercedes-Benz User Experience (MBUX) allows for superior interaction with the world around it, and a closer connection to those inside. All the while, its sporty physique and seductive interior place it in a class all by itself. Learn more at MBUSA.com/GLC

ROLLING STONE (ISSN 0035-791x) is published 12 times per year, which is subject to change at any time, by Penske Business Media, LLC, 475 Fifth Avenue, New York, NY 10017. The entire contents of ROLLING STONE are copyright © 2019 by ROLLING STONE LLC, and may not be reproduced in any manner, either in whole or in part, without written permission. All rights are reserved. International Publications Mail Sales Product Agreement No. 450553. The subscription price is $49.95 for one year. The Canadian subscription price is $69.95 for one year, including GST, payable in advance. Canadian Postmaster: Send address changes and returns to P.O. Box 63, Malton CFC, Mississauga, Ontario L4T 3B5. The foreign subscription price is $99.95 for one year, payable in advance. Periodicals postage paid at New York, NY, and additional mailing offices. Canada Poste publication agreement #40683192. Postmaster: Send address changes to ROLLING STONE Customer Service, P.O. Box 37505, Boone, IA 50037-0505. From time to time, ROLLING STONE may share subscriber information with reputable business partners. For further information about our privacy practices or to opt out of such sharing, please see ROLLING STONE's privacy policy at https://pmc.com/privacy-policy/. You may also write to us at 475 Fifth Avenue, New York, NY 10017. Please include your full name, complete mailing address and the name of the magazine title to which you subscribe.

LOOKIN' GOOD, TASTING GREAT

Great Taste. Only 96 Calories.

MILLER LITE. HOLD TRUE.

Correspondence

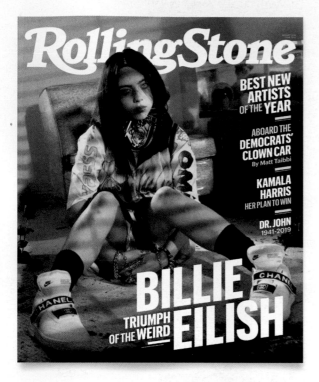

"She's better than 95 percent of pop artists and [did it] without letting the industry decide what she sounds like."

—Mark Gard, via the internet

Billie's Teen Spirit

For Billie Eilish's first ROLLING STONE cover ["Triumph of the Weird," RS 1330], traditional was out of the question. Photographer Petra Collins explained, "There have been a lot of young women on the covers, and I was like, 'I want to do the opposite of what the Britney Spears cover was.'" For reader Rebecca Stout, this resonated. "As a mother of a teenage girl, what can I say but thank you, Billie Eilish, for proving girls don't have to shop their body parts in order to be sexy, cool, or successful." Other readers did not share in this sense of empowerment. "Why the morbid, downer picture of Billie on the cover?" asked Anne Campbell. But for many, it was Eilish's music — not her image — that mattered most. Reader Kevin Dodd wrote, "Eilish's critics need to understand that she and her brother did things on their own. Unlike so many pop artists, they're not the product of record-label commercialism. If we want new music to be creative and uniquely inspired, then we need to support these kinds of performers." Eilish fan Joshua Hess raved, *"When We All Fall Asleep, Where Do We Go?"* is the first album I've listened to start to finish. I've had it on repeat all summer."

 @sarahajeel: I don't think I've ever read a cover story where the opening paragraph is the artist being forced to clean their room!

Dems' Clown Car

Seems like one of the root causes of the circus is the ridiculously long campaign cycle ["The Iowa Circus," RS 1330]. How can we change that?

—Bill MacLeod, via the internet

Goodbye, Dr. John

When I first heard him at 17…as the Night Tripper on *Gris-Gris*, he literally blew the doors off of what I thought music was all about ["The Joy and Mystery of a New Orleans Saint," RS 1330]. There will never be another Dr. John.

—Ian Martin, via the internet

Kamala's Case

Jamil Smith is 100 percent dead-on ["Kamala's Moment," RS 1330]. Love her politics and policies and her campaign. At 62 years old, I made my first political contribution and pledge.

—Phil Panos, via the internet

CONTACT US

Letters to ROLLING STONE, 475 Fifth Avenue, New York, NY 10017-0298. Letters become the property of ROLLING STONE and may be edited for publication. **Email:** letters@rollingstone.com **Subscriber Services:** Call 800-283-1549.

The Kinks in 1964

REUNITED

Fans Debate Kinks Discography

Our Kinks Album Guide was published back in June [RS 1328], but we're still receiving letters from passionate fans taking issue with some of our choices. Many of them found the distinction between "Must-Have" picks like *Village Green Preservation Society* and "Further Listening" selections like *Kinda Kinks* to be rather absurd. "*Arthur* listed as 'Further Listening'?" wrote Christopher Moore. "That's like listing the Beatles' *Rubber Soul* as 'Digging Deeper.'" Kinks fan Reed MacNeilage agreed: "The 'Further Listening' [albums] would be a good career for most bands." Meanwhile, after years of false starts and unfulfilled promises, Ray and Dave Davies are finally recording new songs together and even considering a possible reunion tour, their first since quietly breaking up in 1996. "At this stage, it's far too early to say," Dave recently told ROLLING STONE. "It would be fun, though, wouldn't it?"

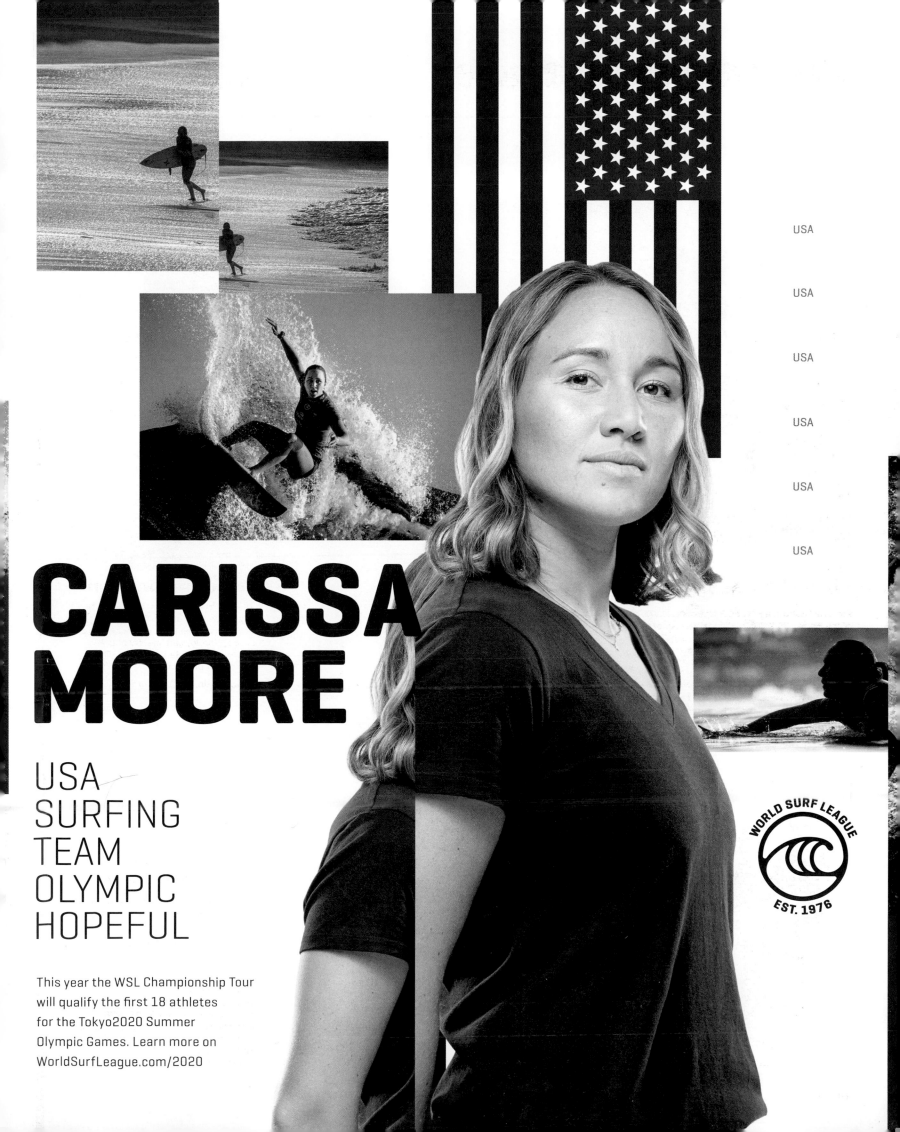

CARISSA MOORE

USA SURFING TEAM OLYMPIC HOPEFUL

This year the WSL Championship Tour will qualify the first 18 athletes for the Tokyo2020 Summer Olympic Games. Learn more on WorldSurfLeague.com/2020

USA

USA

USA

USA

USA

USA

WORLD SURF LEAGUE
EST. 1976

Opening Act

John Mayer's All-Access Pass

JOHN MAYER SPENT the summer touring as a guitarist in Dead and Co. and on his own solo arena run, but he still makes time for his side gig: photography. Mayer has taken his camera on the road for more than a decade. (He prefers a Leica M10, as seen in this portrait.) In 2007, he wrote about his hobby for Nikon's website, and has said he likes to post on photography blogs.

"There's a certain retelling of the truth when you see [your photos]," Mayer has said, adding that he counts Jim Marshall and Annie Leibovitz as his heroes. The guitarist has compared photography to hunting: "Lining up a shot, taking the shot — and [instead of] hanging up what you killed, you hang up what you gave life to." Plus, he said, "It forces you to make more exciting things happen in your life."

Mayer is on his solo tour into October, and he's been taking inspiration from the Grateful Dead. At Madison Square Garden in July, he debuted a cover of "Deal" and thanked the crowd for sticking with him through the rocky parts of his career: "I hope…the people in your life are as patient with you in your coming-of-age…as you have been with me." **PATRICK DOYLE**

Mayer
high above
Australia while
on tour
in March

REAL. SIMPLE. DIFFERENT.

NATURAL
AMERICAN
SPIRIT

TOBACCO INGREDIENTS:
TOBACCO & WATER

We believe in doing things differently.
That's why everything we do is different. From the way our
tobacco is grown to the way we craft our blends.
Tobacco Ingredients: Tobacco & Water

Use your smartphone to check for paperless
Gift Certificates at AmericanSpirit.com*

CIGARETTES

SURGEON GENERAL'S WARNING: Cigarette
Smoke Contains Carbon Monoxide.

Natural American Spirit cigarettes
are not safer than other cigarettes.

Yola's New Town Road

How a British singer reinvented herself, and took over Nashville

ON THE ROAD

Cage & Beck's Big Adventure

Wild sets, big hits: A day in the life of one of the biggest tours of the summer

WHEN CAGE THE ELEPHANT went into the studio to make their first album, singer Matt Shultz had one note for their producer: "'I want to sound like Beck's 'Loser,'" he remembers saying. Now, Cage are touring with their hero on their *Night Running* tour, a double bill that recalls the monster alt-rock tours of the Nineties. "I can't say enough about how blown away I've been," says Shultz of Beck, who's been opening with "Loser" before blasting through uptempo classics like "Devil's Haircut." Cage are drawing heavily from their dark, New Wave-y new album, *Social Cues,* with a high-concept performance that has Shultz stripping seven layers of clothing off his body throughout the set. "I'm trying to show people that I'm loved no matter what state I'm in, whether I'm covered in layers or completely naked," he says. PATRICK DOYLE

BACK TO THE SHACK
Above: Matt arrives at an intimate radio performance at Chicago's Reggies. "We do one of those every day," says Brad.

UNCAGED
"He's tapping into something right now that's bigger than our band," says Brad Shultz of his brother Matt. "It's inspiring."

➔ YOLA

IT WAS HARD to miss Yola at July's Newport Folk Festival. The brightly dressed, earthy-voiced singer appeared on multiple stages at the legendary Rhode Island event, dropping in on sets by the Highwomen – where she got the biggest cheers of the supergroup's show – and Dolly Parton, who welcomed Yola for a raucous group singalong of "9 to 5." She also drew an overflowing crowd to her own side-stage performance, delivering a deeply moving set of country-soul originals. "Yola is a force unlike any we've ever seen in this genre," says Brandi Carlile, who considers Yola an "honorary member" of her group Highwomen.

This kind of thing has been happening a lot this year, since the 36-year-old released *Walk Through Fire.* Her debut LP combines the lush heartbreak of Sixties torch songs with Nashville rootsiness, telling the story of a deeply painful relationship and how the singer-songwriter got out of it. (See "Walk Through Fire," where Yola sings, "My bags are packed, and I'm ready/I think I'm gonna make a run, oh, Lord.") The album earned her an opening slot on the latest leg of Kacey Musgraves' "Oh, What a World" Tour –

FAST FACTS

ALL I WANNA DO
The first artist she ever covered, at age 14, was Sheryl Crow, whom Yola recently joined onstage.

20 FEET FROM STARDOM As a backup singer, she worked with Ludacris and the Chemical Brothers.

when Musgraves made the announcement, she called Yola an "icon." "Every other day, something really awesome has been happening," Yola says. "It feels totally abnormal."

Yola's breakthrough comes after years of what she calls "being kept in my box." She grew up in Bristol, England, and had a strained relationship with her mother, who died in 2013. (Yola attributes the tension, in part, to her mother's "traits of psychopathy.") After graduating from a "demifancy" grammar school she attended on scholarship, Yola became involved with London's dance-music scene. Over the next decade, she lived several musical lives: as a top-

PHOTOGRAPHS BY **Sacha Lecca**

ELEPHANT HERD
The band – Daniel Tichenor, Brad, Jared Champion, Matt, Nick Bockrath, Matthan Minster – outside their club show at Reggies.

SURF'S UP
Below: Matt surfs to the end of the floor. "Some of the things he does scare the hell out of me," says Brad of his brother.

CAFFEINE FIEND
Below: Brad arriving at the radio show: "I was drinking 14 [espresso] shots a day and had a barista intervention. My coffee shop said, "Are you sure you should be drinking this much?'" Left: Beck with Matt.

UNDER COVER
Left: Matt strips off seven layers during each Cage set, though all that fabric can be challenging at the start of a gig: "When I start to struggle, some people are mortified."

MIDNIGHT VULTURES
Right: Matt and Beck team up for "Where It's At." Brad was shocked when Beck recently offered to ship them recording equipment: "It's like a childhood dream."

line songwriter, an uncredited vocalist on a few massive British dance-music hits, and as the lead singer for folk-rock band Phantom Limb. She did some work as a backup singer, though she turned down an offer to work with Adele. "People try to coax you into those jobs all the time as a woman of color," says Yola. "Backup singers are almost ubiquitously my shade or darker. The moment I touch it, I devalue my voice."

Yola felt a similar lack of creative control in her band Phantom Limb, which led her to quit the group in 2013. She took a three-year break from music, funded by royalty checks from British club tracks she sang on

"Every other day, something really awesome has been happening," says Yola of the past year. "It feels totally abnormal."

and produced. "My life looked like this," she says. "Tuesday: tennis. Thursday: javelin. Saturday: horse-riding. In the middle: loads of cocktails and eating in a kind of super-gastronomically-advanced way."

As a way to make sense of her tumultuous time in Phantom Limb, Yola began writing new kinds of songs: more honest and raw, about "the hurt of divorcing myself from that [time]." She thought about all the relationships – personally and musically – where she felt relegated to a supporting role. "For quite a long time, I put on the 'I can do anything, I'm a strong black woman' bullshit," Yola says. "But all that does is reinforce a

paradigm of neglect. And you get pushed into it a lot more if you're in white spaces most of your life, which I was."

The latest space she's learned to navigate is Nashville, where she recorded *Walk Through Fire* with producer Dan Auerbach (of the Black Keys), and now stays in a space owned by fellow Americana artist Rhiannon Giddens. Yola is still getting used to all the acclaim – for an album she made entirely on her own terms. "The response has made me highly emotional," she says. "Getting tweeted by Kendall Jenner and Jamie Lee Curtis was not on the list of things I expected for this record." JONATHAN BERNSTEIN

PLAYLIST

OUR FAVORITE SONGS AND VIDEOS RIGHT NOW

1. Charli XCX
"Cross You Out"

The punky U.K. pop diva is releasing her first LP in five years, full of confrontationally weird party jams like this emo collabo with fellow rules hater Sky Ferreira. Over a stomping, synth-glazed groove, they detonate the memory of an ex, creating their own killer moment of sisterly chaos.

2. DaBaby and Lil Baby
"Baby"

Lil Baby's *Drip Harder* was one of our favorite hip-hop albums of 2018, and DaBaby's *Baby on Baby* is one of our favorites from this year. What can we say? It's a good time for rappers named Baby, as their frenetically banging tag-team "Baby" attests.

3. Vivian Girls
"Sick"

The Vivian Girls make sweetly bracing indie pop somewhere between the Go-Go's and My Bloody Valentine, and they're finally back after a way-too-long eight-year hiatus.

4. Miranda Lambert
"It All Comes Out in the Wash"

Ever brought a bridesmaid's ex to a wedding? Ever accidentally told your mama that your sister got knocked up in a truck outside 7-Eleven? Hey, it happens. And the country queen's latest blast of wry, rocking wisdom is the perfect antidote to the stains and aches of everyday life — a Tide stick for the soul.

5. Velvet Negroni
"Wine Green"

A Minnesotan raised on classical music and evangelical Christianity, Jeremy Nutzman (a.k.a. Velvet Negroni) blurs art pop, R&B, and dub into something uniquely weird and delicately gorgeous. Keep an eye on this dude.

6. Ariana Grande and Social House
"Boyfriend"

The generosity of "Thank U, Next" is nowhere to be found on Grande's new breakup jam: "I don't want to miss your touch/ And you don't seem to give a fuck," she sings, reminding us why her "train wreck" is pop's top drama.

7. Diiv
"Skin Game"

These noise junkies do Nineties shoegaze with the creepily obsessive dedication of Civil War re-enactors — and it sure does work.

8. Bonny Light Horseman
"Bonny Light Horseman"

Anaïs Mitchell, author of the Tony-winning musical *Hadestown*, fronts this fine new folk band, channeling an ancient ache on its first single.

9. Haim
"Summer Girl"

Written to send good vibes to their producer, Ariel Rechtshaid, who had contracted cancer, Haim came up with a jazzy pick-you-up, pulling back their sleek Eighties sound to highlight its tender core.

10. Anuel AA, Daddy Yankee, Karol G, Ozuna, and J Balvin
"China"

A veritable Justice League of Latin pop convenes for a Spanish-language cover of Shaggy's reggae-pop classic "It Wasn't Me," and mind-breaking catchiness ensues.

For reviews, premieres, and more, go to Rolling Stone.com/music

---

MY LIST

FIVE SONGS THAT SHAPED ME

By Thurston Moore

The former Sonic Youth singer-guitarist is releasing the three-CD box set *Spirit Counsel* on September 21st and touring America in December.

PATTI SMITH
"Godspeed"

This is a stream-of-conscious piece of music that sounds like it was done in the middle of the night with the lights out.

MINOR THREAT
"In My Eyes"

There's a rage in the vocal delivery here that is undeniable. It's taking on a youth culture that believes in the lies of capitalist society.

BUSH TETRAS
"Too Many Creeps"

This is about these girls walking around New York dealing with creepy guys. It's punk mixed with hip-hop, jazz, and salsa vibes.

GLENN BRANCA
"Lesson #1 for Electric Guitar"

Glenn is one of my biggest influences. This is an instrumental guitar piece that helped inform a lot of what I did in Sonic Youth.

TAPPER ZUKIE
"Man ah Warrior"

This is reggae music, but really stripped back. It's just intonation and the clack of a guitar pick on the strings. Tapper Zukie is cooler than cool.

REAL APPRECIATION

ISN'T SPOKEN, IT'S POURED.

JIM BEAM
BLACK

MUSIC

Charli's Weird-Pop Reinvention

In the six-year "break" between Charli XCX's *Sucker* and *Charli* (out September 13th), she put out mixtapes, an EP, and six solo releases – *and* teamed up with Taylor Swift, Shawn Mendes, and Camila Cabello. Now, Charli's back from her working vacation and getting serious(-ish). "It's fun to write songs about cars," she says of *Charli*. "But I began to analyze my emotional state." Here's how she got it done. BRITTANY SPANOS

Let It Get Weird

In 2014, Charli's career blew up, set off by a trio of pop hits: "Fancy" with Iggy Azalea, solo single "Boom Clap," and omnipresent Icona Pop collaboration "I Love It." "But did it" — "it" meaning "global success" — "make me feel fulfilled artistically?" Charli asks. "No." So for her third album, she stopped worrying and embraced the odd. On dissonantly Auto-Tuned songs like "Click" and "Next Level Charli," she leans into the organized electronic chaos introduced on mixtape *Pop 2*. "I'm not thinking, 'Is this too weird?'" Charli says. "I don't care that it's not going to get on the radio."

Make Music You Can Party To

The last album Charli released wasn't up to her standards in one crucial way. "Even though I'm very proud of *Sucker*," she says, "I knew I wasn't making the ultimate music I wanted to hear when I was partying." So this spring, she and PC Music founder A.G. Cook spent eight weeks recording that ultimate music in Los Angeles. How did they start the Charli party? "We were like, 'Fuck it,'" she says. "'Let's do it.'"

It's Better Together

Christine and the Queens co-wrote verses for new single "Gone." Troye Sivan repartnered with Charli for their "1999" follow-up, "2099," because, she says she told him, "I love you and I love that song, but now we have to do something for the gays." And when she came up with stark New Wave jam "Cross You Out," it was the perfect excuse to finally hook up with Sky Ferreira. (The pair have shared magazine covers and stages since meeting as teens, but never released a song together.) For Charli, collaborating is a master class: "I learn so much."

Expose Your Tender Underbelly

In a fit of self-awareness, Charli realized she saw music as a competitive sport. "Sometimes I think I'm better than every one of you, and other times I feel like I'm literally nothing," she says of her place in the industry. "There's so much pressure to be the funniest and know your brand and be the wokest and not upset anyone, but also be provocative. I don't have to feel like that superhero all the time."

ASK CROZ

Real-life advice from a guy who's seen, done, and survived just about everything

---

I have been clean from cocaine and heroin for a year, and I think I can start smoking some pot. What's a good strain to keep from getting back on the coke and smack?

—Mark, Alamosa, CO

As if there were a strain for that, you nincompoop! Coke and heroin take you over the way fire takes over a building. For me, it was 10 years before the slip dreams stopped and I was pretty sure it wasn't snapping at my heels anymore – and I waited almost five years after *that* before I smoked pot. Give yourself some time with sobriety.

What advice would you give about living with the existential dread of being a hippie in America? I'm as gentle as Mister Rogers, but because of my appearance and the associations it brings, I've faced intimidation in certain situations.

—Carl Thomas Hriczak, Niagara Falls, NY

Have any black friends? They'll tell you all about it. I think it's very educational for a white person in the American scene to be treated like a second-class citizen. Rather than resenting it or trying to avoid it, you should experience and learn from it.

I'm a professor at a small liberal-arts college. A beautiful young woman in my class was very flirty with me throughout the semester, and now the class is over. Would I be a fool to invite her to dinner?

—Name Withheld

You're holding all the power. It bends the relationship. And, to use an old expression, don't shit where you eat. It'll compromise your relationship with that student, and with all your other students, who are watching and will know. If you're a teacher, you have a role to play. It doesn't involve taking someone out and trying to get her in bed.

GOT A QUESTION FOR CROZ?
Email AskCroz@Rollingstone.com

PHOTOGRAPH BY **Griffin Lotz**

ILLUSTRATION BY LARS LEETARU

HIGHLY SUSPECT

NEW ALBUM

11.01.19

300

CHECKING IN

What Scares Stephen King?

His new book predicted Trump's horrors, and he has a lot more on the way. The only thing he doesn't want to think about? Retirement

By ANDY GREENE

DONALD TRUMP was still months away from being elected president when Stephen King began writing his upcoming novel. But *The Institute* – out September 10th and centered on a 12-year-old boy stolen from

The Institute
By Stephen King
Scribner
"I wanted to write a book like *Tom Brown's School Days*," King says. "But in hell."

his parents in the night and locked up in a mysterious facility – is likely to remind readers of certain immigration policies. "I can't help but see similarity between what's going on in *The Institute* and those pictures of kids in cages," says King. "Sometimes fiction outpaces fact."

This isn't the first time a King book predicted the political future: His 1979 book *The Dead Zone* was about a Trump-like aspiring president threatening global apocalypse if he took office. "Fiction has foreseen Trump before," says King, "always as a nightmare. Now, the nightmare is here. But I don't want to force my worldview on people. I'm not George Orwell, and this book isn't *1984*."

King is calling in from his house in Maine, just a couple of weeks after traveling to

> King in New York last year

> **"I'll either collapse at my desk or the ideas will run out – the thing you don't want to do is embarrass yourself."**

Foxborough, Massachusetts, to see his first-ever Rolling Stones concert. ("Keith looked a little tentative and just putting in the time at first, but then he caught fire.") He's still reveling in the surge of interest in his work that followed 2017's *It*, now the highest-grossing horror movie ever. "I think a lot of kids watched the [1990] *It* miniseries with Tim Curry, and it scared the living shit

right out of them," King says. "They couldn't wait to go back and see it again."

Like *It*, *The Institute* is about a group of children who band together to battle an unspeakably evil force. The twist this time is that they all have telekinetic or psychic powers and the adults who run the facility force them to undergo medical experiments. "I wanted to write a book like *Tom Brown's*

School Days," King says, referencing the 1857 Thomas Hughes children's classic about a British boarding school. "But in hell."

A book about clairvoyant kids battling a shadow organization will surely draw comparisons to *Stranger Things*. Which was, of course, heavily inspired by Stephen King books. "I think it does owe something to *It*," the author says. "Another book

about kids who are weak and helpless by themselves – but together can make something that is very strong."

The Institute could be the next King project to be adapted by Hollywood, joining *The Stand* (CBS All Access), *Castle Rock* (Hulu), and many other TV series – plus the seven movies he has in development, including *It Chapter 2*. King has script approval on all of them. "They have to work," he says. "It can't have 19 pages of flashbacks to when the characters were kids. I want the pedal to the metal as much of the time as possible."

The film adaptation of King's 2013 *The Shining* sequel, *Dr. Sleep*, comes out November 8th and features Ewan McGregor playing an adult Danny Torrance. Though King has always hated Stanley Kubrick's 1980 adaptation of his book for changing so much of the story, he allowed the *Dr. Sleep* filmmakers to use elements of Kubrick's version. "My problem with Kubrick's film was that it's so cold," King says. "The reason I didn't have any problem with this script is they took some of Kubrick's material and warmed it up."

King's next book, *If It Bleeds*, is another in his ongoing Holly Gibney detective series and is due sometime in 2020. He's already working on the novel that will follow. "I'm 71 years old," King says, "and a lot of people my age are forgotten. I've had this late-season burst of success. It's very gratifying."

Naturally, retirement remains the last thing on his mind. "That's God's decision, not mine," he says. "I'll either collapse at my desk or the ideas will run out – the thing you don't want to do is embarrass yourself. As long as I feel like I'm still doing good work, I can't see myself stopping." Ⓡ

NICOTINE
SATISFACTION
CRAFTED FOR SMOKERS

Cigarettes are simple.

With myblu-vaping can be too.

- All-day charge
- Easy to use pre-filled pods
- Widest selection of flavors

Learn more at **MYBLU.COM**

©2019 Fontem. NOT FOR SALE TO MINORS.

DEVICE

my blu™

Device + USB Charger
LIQUIDPODS SOLD SEPARATELY

blu.com

Aerosmith in 2018

①TRAIN
②DUDE
THE OTHER SIDE
RAG DOLL
LAST CHILD
③SWEET EMOTION
④HANGMAN
SEASONS
⑤STOP MESSIN'
⑥CRYIN'
⑦EDGE
THIGHS
WHAT IT TAKES
ELEVATOR
⑧TOYS
⑨DREAM ON
⑩CHIP AWAY
⑪WALK THIS WAY

PARK MGM VEGAS RESIDENCY – VERS

ON THE ROAD

Aerosmith Tell Their Set List Secrets

During their Vegas residency, band members break down how they play a killer set

By ANDY GREENE

1. Train Kept A-Rollin' 1974

This blues standard (popularized by the Yardbirds) was one of the first songs Aerosmith learned. "To play it now and see audiences react the same way they did back then," Steven Tyler says, "it's a euphoric recall."

2. Dude (Looks Like a Lady) 1987

Tyler wrote these lyrics about an androgynous man after spending time with Vince Neil. "A lot of people know it from *Mrs. Doubtfire*," says guitarist Brad Whitford. "It's a crowd favorite."

3. Sweet Emotion 1975

For years, Aerosmith saved their breakthrough hit for the end of the show. Lately, they've been trying it earlier. "In Vegas, we can only play for an hour and a half," says Tyler, "so we have to make sure we fit in all our hits."

4. Hangman Jury 1987

Tyler and Joe Perry play this raw blues stomper while seated on chairs deep within the crowd. "It's like they're jamming on a front porch," says bassist Tom Hamilton.

5. Stop Messin' Around 2004

This Fleetwood Mac cover gives Perry a chance to sing lead. "Joe sings his ass off," says Tyler. "It's a tip of the hat to the band that made me want to join Aerosmith: Fleetwood Mac."

6. Cryin' 1993

The video for this massive hit featured an unknown Alicia Silverstone. "This isn't one of my favorites," says Hamilton. "I wouldn't mind giving it a rest."

7. Livin' on the Edge 1993

Tyler wrote this song after witnessing the 1992 L.A. riots. "Those lyrics will be appropriate from now until the end of eternity," says Hamilton.

8. Toys in the Attic 1975

The main set wraps up with one of the fastest songs in their catalog. "It gets the crowd pumped up before we walk off," says Whitford.

9. Dream On 1973

They've played this power ballad more than 1,500 times and can't imagine a show without it. "It damn near wrote itself," says Tyler. "I think it's lasted as long as it has because the message stands the test of time. Oh, and because of that scream…"

10. Chip Away the Stone 1978

In between their biggest hits, Aerosmith break out this obscure Seventies singalong. "It's kind of a 'Brown Sugar'-like song," says Hamilton. Adds Tyler, "It got a lot of airplay during the days of AOR: album-oriented rock."

11. Walk This Way 1975

"There's so much history with that song," says Whitford. "It was just enormous, and it's the perfect closer."

Aerosmith return to the MGM Grand on September 21st, and play there through December.

RS PICKS

ARTIST PODCASTS

Legends share wild tales, song secrets in new shows

David Lee Roth

THE ROTH SHOW
The Van Halen singer is like an insane late-night talk-radio DJ, telling stories and philosophizing on everything from the relationship between drumming and boxing to how the buttless pants he wore in 1983 launched Shakira's career. He delivers each weirdly intimate ramble with the same over-the-top energy that made him Eighties metal's greatest frontman.

Robert Plant

DIGGING DEEP
In each episode of his fascinating show, Plant zeros in on one song from his career. Example: "Achilles Last Stand," where he breaks down how a serious car-accident injury led him to write a track he admits is "magnificent…so intense." "It's not self-indulgent," Plant said of his show. "It's basically *hugely* indulgent."

Aimee Mann and Ted Leo

THE ART OF PROCESS
The two thoughtful indie songwriters (who also perform together as the Both) host talks on the artistic process with an eclectic group, from rapper Jean Grae to political speechwriter Eli Attie. Each episode offers a deep look into the passions and anxieties that fuel creativity.

BIRKENSTOCK®

Tradition since 1774.

Tricia and Terry Jones — i–D original mum and founding editor,
wearing her silver metallic *Madrid*, purchased in 2004, and his brown suede
Arizona, purchased in 1993. Photographed in Somerset, 2019.

Lil Baby in
Atlanta in July

Lil Baby: An Atlanta Rap Star Is Born

Three years ago, the rapper was in prison. Now he's racking up billions of streams and getting VIP service at his favorite deli

LIL BABY IS one of the year's biggest breakout stars, scoring 9 billion streams and a Best New Artist win at the BET Awards. "Every day, I got a new accomplishment," says the 24-year-old Atlanta rapper. Today's accomplishment: picking up the 10-piece extra-crispy chicken from his hometown's American Deli. Lil Baby's been frequenting the spot since childhood, where a longtime employee whom Baby calls "Auntie" has his order ready when he walks in. ("She was a big fan before I started rapping," he says.) Lil Baby's hip-hop career began in 2017, after he spent years in and out of prison and juvenile detention. Baby quickly distinguished himself with melodic, aggressive songs about his life in Atlanta ("TSA harass me, so I took a private plane," he raps on "Drip Too Hard"). Now Lil Baby is recording the follow-up to his Top 10 album, *Harder Than Ever,* at late-night sessions that usually start after his two sons go to sleep. "I came out [of prison] with a different mindset that has turned me into who I am today," Lil Baby says. "I'm shooting for the sky." ANGIE MARTOCCIO

IMPORTANT FACTS ABOUT TRUVADA (tru-VAH-dah)

This is only a brief summary of important information about taking TRUVADA for PrEP. This does not replace talking to your healthcare provider about your medicine.

Truvada®
emtricitabine 200 mg / tenofovir
disoproxil fumarate 300 mg tablets
for **PrEP** pre-exposure prophylaxis

MOST IMPORTANT INFORMATION

ABOUT TRUVADA FOR PrEP

Before starting and while taking TRUVADA for PrEP:
- **You must be HIV negative.** Do not take TRUVADA for PrEP to reduce the risk of getting HIV-1 unless you are confirmed to be HIV-negative. Get tested for HIV immediately before and at least every 3 months while taking TRUVADA. If you think you were exposed to HIV, tell your healthcare provider right away.
- **Many HIV tests can miss HIV infection in a person who has recently become infected.** Symptoms of new HIV infection include tiredness, fever, joint or muscle aches, headache, sore throat, vomiting, diarrhea, rash, night sweats, and/or enlarged lymph nodes in the neck or groin. Tell your healthcare provider if you have had these symptoms or a flu-like illness within the last month before starting or while taking TRUVADA.
- **You must continue to use safer sex practices. Just taking TRUVADA for PrEP may not keep you from getting HIV.** Do not miss any doses of TRUVADA. Missing doses may increase your risk of getting HIV.
- **If you do become HIV-positive, you need more medicine than TRUVADA alone to treat HIV.** TRUVADA by itself is not a complete treatment for HIV. If you have HIV and take only TRUVADA, your HIV may become harder to treat now and in the future.

TRUVADA may cause serious side effects, including:
- **Worsening of hepatitis B (HBV) infection.** Your healthcare provider will test you for HBV. If you have HBV and stop taking TRUVADA, your HBV may suddenly get worse. Do not stop taking TRUVADA without first talking to your healthcare provider, as they will need to check your health regularly for several months.

ABOUT TRUVADA FOR PrEP

TRUVADA for PrEP is a prescription medicine that can help reduce the risk of getting HIV-1 through sex, when taken every day and used together with safer sex practices. This use is only for people who weigh at least 77 pounds and are HIV-negative and at risk of getting HIV.
- To help determine your risk of getting HIV-1, talk openly with your healthcare provider about your sexual health.

Do NOT take TRUVADA for PrEP if you:
- **Already have HIV infection or if you do not know your HIV status.** TRUVADA by itself is not a complete treatment for HIV. If you have HIV and take only TRUVADA, your HIV may become harder to treat now and in the future.

Tell your healthcare provider if you:
- Have or have had any kidney, bone, or liver problems, including hepatitis.
- Have any other medical conditions.
- Are pregnant or plan to become pregnant. It is not known if TRUVADA can harm your unborn baby. If you become pregnant while taking TRUVADA for PrEP, tell your healthcare provider.
- Are breastfeeding (nursing) or plan to breastfeed. Do not breastfeed if you think you may have recently become infected with HIV. HIV can pass to the baby in breast milk. Talk to your healthcare provider about the risks and benefits of breastfeeding while taking TRUVADA for PrEP.

Tell your healthcare provider about all the medicines you take:
- Keep a list that includes all prescription and over-the-counter medicines, vitamins, and herbal supplements, and show it to your healthcare provider and pharmacist.
- Ask your healthcare provider or pharmacist about medicines that should not be taken with TRUVADA for PrEP.
- If you take certain other medicines with TRUVADA, your healthcare provider may need to check you more often or change your dose. These medicines include certain medicines to treat hepatitis B or C infection.

POSSIBLE SIDE EFFECTS OF TRUVADA FOR PrEP

TRUVADA may cause serious side effects, including:
- Those in the "Most Important Information About TRUVADA for PrEP" section.
- **New or worse kidney problems, including kidney failure.** Your healthcare provider should do blood and urine tests to check your kidneys before and during treatment with TRUVADA. If you develop kidney problems, your healthcare provider may tell you to stop taking TRUVADA.
- **Too much lactic acid in your blood (lactic acidosis),** which is a serious but rare medical emergency that can lead to death. Tell your healthcare provider right away if you get these symptoms: weakness or being more tired than usual, unusual muscle pain, being short of breath or fast breathing, stomach pain with nausea and vomiting, cold or blue hands and feet, feel dizzy or lightheaded, or a fast or abnormal heartbeat.
- **Severe liver problems,** which in rare cases can lead to death. Tell your healthcare provider right away if you get these symptoms: skin or the white part of your eyes turns yellow, dark "tea-colored" urine, light-colored stools, loss of appetite for several days or longer, nausea, or stomach-area pain.
- **Bone problems,** including bone pain, softening, or thinning, which may lead to fractures. Your healthcare provider may do tests to check your bones.

Common side effects in people taking TRUVADA for PrEP include headache, stomach-area (abdomen) pain, and decreased weight.

These are not all the possible side effects of TRUVADA. Tell your healthcare provider right away if you have any new symptoms while taking TRUVADA for PrEP.

You are encouraged to report negative side effects of prescription drugs to the FDA. Visit www.FDA.gov/medwatch, or call 1-800-FDA-1088.

Your healthcare provider will need to do tests to monitor your health before and during treatment with TRUVADA for PrEP.

HOW TO TAKE TRUVADA FOR PrEP

- **Take 1 tablet once a day, every day,** not just when you think you have been exposed to HIV-1.
- Do not miss any doses. Missing doses may increase your risk of getting HIV-1 infection.
- Use TRUVADA for PrEP together with safer sex practices.
- Get tested for HIV-1 at least every 3 months. You must stay HIV-negative to keep taking TRUVADA for PrEP.

HOW TO FURTHER REDUCE YOUR RISK

- Know your HIV status and the HIV status of your partners. If your partner is living with HIV, your risk of getting HIV is lower if your partner consistently takes HIV treatment every day.
- Get tested for other sexually transmitted infections. Other infections make it easier for HIV to infect you.
- Practice safer sex by using latex or polyurethane condoms.
- Talk to your healthcare provider about all the ways to help reduce HIV risk.

GET MORE INFORMATION

- This is only a brief summary of important information about TRUVADA for PrEP. Talk to your healthcare provider or pharmacist to learn more, including how to prevent HIV infection.
- Go to TRUVADA.com or call 1-800-GILEAD-5
- If you need help paying for your medicine, visit TRUVADA.com for program information.

BEHIND THE SCENES

Harper, Jacinto, Danson, Carden, Bell, and Jamil (from left)

TV's Most Divine Comedy

Goodbye to 'The Good Place,' which taught us ethics and was hilarious at the same time

By ALAN SEPINWALL

IT'S HOT as hell on the set of *The Good Place*.

The wickedly smart NBC comedy about a group of misfits struggling to make their way through the afterlife largely takes place in its

THE GOOD PLACE
Season Four premieres September 26th
at 9 p.m. on NBC

own version of Satan's domain. The show's central neighborhood looks like a pastel paradise filled with shops that have punny names like The Pesto's Yet to Come and Lasagna Come Out Tomorrow. But it's built on the Universal backlot in the San Fernando Valley, which can feel like the sun's anvil as production hits the summer months. Between takes while shooting the series' upcoming fourth and final season, leading lady Kristen Bell tries to explain the concepts of "swamp ass" and "monkey butt" – "It's just a general stickiness" – to legendary co-star Ted Danson, and each time a crew member orders the cast to step out of the sun, Bell and D'Arcy Carden harmonize on a lyric from *Dear Evan Hansen* about doing exactly that.

"It would be an accurate temperature in hell," Bell acknowledges later from the comfort of her trailer. "Maybe this is part of [*Good Place* creator] Mike Schur's big plan. I wouldn't put it past him."

Through its first three seasons, *The Good Place* has pushed the limits of where a sitcom can go – physically, metaphysically, stylistically, and philosophically. It began in what appeared to be an exclusive version of heaven, where four newly arrived human dum-dums – selfish con artist Eleanor (Bell), indecisive philosopher Chidi (William Jackson Harper), narcissistic philanthropist Tahani (Jameela Jamil), and "Florida Man" Jason (Manny Jacinto) – didn't seem to quite fit, despite encouragement from gregarious celestial architect Michael (Danson) and chipperly omniscient artificial intelligence Janet (Carden). In a twist that was kept secret from all the actors save Danson and Bell – and that transformed *The Good Place* from clever sitcom to something addictive – they would learn that Michael was actually a Bad Place demon testing out a new way to torture souls. The flummoxed foursome would spend the ensuing seasons trying to save themselves from eternal damnation and figure out why the universe seems utterly broken. (A recent episode revealed that no one has qualified for the Good Place in centuries.) Silly as it can be, the series asks big questions about the best way to live, how to treat the world and peo-ple around us, and how to cope in a life that seems more profoundly unfair by the year. This surreal show filled with impossibilities such as lava monsters, genies, and giant flying shrimp has turned out to be an essential guide for staying sane in the age of Trump.

"This and *The Handmaid's Tale* are two documentaries about the time we're living in," says frequent guest star Marc Evan Jackson (he plays the snippy demon Shawn, the bureaucrat honcho of the Bad Place), only half-kidding.

"It's about what it means to lead a decent life and that there are consequences to our actions," says Danson. "So it's a really wonderful, ethical conversation. And there's a lot of nine-year-old fart humor interspersed to make that go down. And there's lots of visual magic to make it all sparkly."

The existence of *The Good Place* on TV at all, much less on a traditional broadcast network, feels as unlikely as an atheist would feel about the af-

PHOTOGRAPH BY **Kelia Anne**

terlife itself. But after the success of *Parks and Recreation* and *Brooklyn Nine-Nine,* creator Schur was offered a rare opportunity in television.

"This all started," he recalls, "from NBC doing something insane, which was telling me that they would take any idea I had and guarantee it 13 episodes. And what I took from that offer was, 'Well, I now owe it to the concept of ideas to come up with a crazy idea.' Why play it safe in that scenario?"

Schur was already fixated on notions of fairness and ethics. He first developed the show's concept of a point system to get into the Good Place while fighting L.A. traffic and deducting or adding points for other drivers based on how they behaved on the road. He found it was a fascination he shared with Bell, with whom he'd worked briefly on *Parks.*

"It's something I think about a lot,"

(electric vans or solar power whenever possible, no plastic water bottles) extreme even for a Hollywood set.

Writer Megan Amram says the writers room can get intense: "We talk at length about death, what it means to be a good person, and how we are genuinely trying to change our day-to-day lives to be better people. We sucked so bad when we started the show, and now we're all vegetarians. It's great."

Jamil has stopped killing insects, and admits her behavior is now influenced by Schur's point system. "You never come to Hollywood and become a better person," she says. "That's not the way it's supposed to be."

IN ANOTHER ERA, a show about ethics would have been a harder sell, but this one happened to debut in the fall of 2016. "It didn't hurt that from the moment the show

would devote entire seasons to, just to keep viewers excited and engaged.

"The show is incredibly optimistic and snarky," suggests Harper. In other shows right now, "if there's optimism or any sort of openheartedness, it lacks bite. And if it has a lot of bite, it's just completely devoid of any heart. And I feel like our show has a really good meshing of the two."

The series has its own in-house visual-effects wizard, David Niednagel, to bring the writers' strange inventions to life. But Danson himself supplies at least as much of the magic with a performance that's everything Schur asks of him and more: otherworldly but also deeply childlike and vulnerable, cartoonish but also capable of intense, admirable humanity. Carden jumps back in her chair and grips the armrests recalling the creepy laugh Danson improvised in the scene where

Danson once famously opted to end *Cheers* for fear it would grow stale. Now he finds himself on the receiving end of a similar choice by Schur, who chose to make this upcoming fourth season *The Good Place*'s last, having told his sprawling story at warp speed. It's a decision everyone understands, even as none of them want to let go.

"I think we don't know how lucky we are," says Danson. "I'm really proud to have been part of it. It's a great conversation to be had. And the fact that 11- and 12-year-olds are coming up loving the show, to me that's when kids are just starting to turn their headlights on and they're understanding humor and they're impressionable and smart. So if they like the show, we're doing something right."

"I suppose I feel exactly the way it would feel at the end of your life," says Bell. "I know it has to end, but I didn't

FROM 'SNL' TO 'THE GOOD PLACE'
For more than two decades, writer-producer Mike Schur has crafted some of TV's finest sitcoms and sketches. Here, a few of his greatest hits

SATURDAY NIGHT LIVE
WRITER, 1997-2004
Though focused on "Weekend Update" and politics (see Al Gore and George W. Bush as *The Odd Couple*), he co-wrote the "Turd Ferguson Celebrity Jeopardy" skit.

THE OFFICE
WRITER-PRODUCER, 2005-2007
Schur wrote many memorable early episodes like "Office Olympics" and "Christmas Party" — and wore a neckbeard to play Dwight's weird cousin Mose.

PARKS AND RECREATION
SHOWRUNNER, 2009-2015
He teamed with *Office* boss Greg Daniels and Amy Poehler to create the sweetly hilarious ode to public service that made stars of Chris Pratt, Aziz Ansari, and more.

BROOKLYN NINE-NINE
SHOWRUNNER, 2013-PRESENT
When Fox canceled the endearingly goofy cop show starring Andy Samberg and Andre Braugher last year, the outcry was so great, NBC rescued it a day later.

Bell says. "Not one person owns Earth. We're here together, one big family, whether we want to admit it or not. And in a family, people have to cooperate or it's dysfunctional. How do you do that? Are there rules? Should there be? Who has ideas about the rules?"

Schur tries to practice what the show preaches. He's long had a "no assholes" rule on his sets, unusual in a business where bad behavior is often indulged as the alleged price of great art. The writing staff regularly consults with philosophy professors for story ideas. (Harper, who as Chidi has to explain most of the show's ethical concepts to the audience, admits he often turns to Wikipedia for a basic grasp of them, because he finds key *Good Place* texts like T.M. Scanlon's *What We Owe to Each Other* too dense.) The show's themes have gradually infected most of the cast and crew. Producers have instituted a series of green policies

aired," Schur notes, "the word 'ethics' was appearing in every newspaper on Earth every day."

"I think we're craving positive entertainment now," argues Bell, highlighting one of the few upsides of America's ongoing sociopolitical malaise. "Eight years ago, five years ago, when the world felt safer, it felt OK to root for an antihero. Walter White was awesome, because the world felt safer, right? Now, the world feels unsafe, and I don't think people want to turn the television on to that. I think they want to see people fighting for good."

None of this would matter if the show weren't so forking (to borrow Eleanor's profanity workaround that keeps her from cussing in the afterlife) funny and inventive at every turn. There's a density of jokes in every scene that the actors find inspiring. The writers use and discard plot ideas in a single episode that most shows

Eleanor figures out that she and her friends are really in the Bad Place. She and all of Danson's other co-stars light up when talking about how humble and genuinely curious he still is, in a way that goes beyond normal Hollywood platitudes about how everyone in the cast is a family.

"He's just kind of joy personified," says Bell. "He's witty, and he's happy from the moment he wakes up until about 3 p.m. And then he gets sleepy."

Jamil had never acted before being cast and was terrified during the filming of her first scene, where Michael introduces Eleanor to Tahani. To break the tension, she says, Danson "just kept on pretending to fart on me. Which was so weird but brilliant, and just made me feel so instantly comfortable. He kept making himself seem as little and silly as humanly possible, because he could tell that I was awestruck by him."

quite get enough and I want a little more." At 39, with two little kids at home, Bell is thinking about taking a step back from work. "Maybe this is a great note to go out on," she suggests. "I'll do a movie here or there, or be a guest star, but maybe I won't be number one on the call sheet anymore."

It's hardest on the less-experienced cast. "I am unemployed, so if you have anything, please let me know," Jacinto jokes. "I can wash your car."

Through her infectious performance as the all-knowing, all-powerful, always-optimistic Janet, Carden may embody the series more than anyone. She gets choked up just thinking about the conclusion of her big break.

"You want to hear something really cheesy?" she asks. "If you really think about it, if someone were to design my Good Place, it would be this. It sucks that now my Good Place is ending. But it's good, it's good. It's right." Ⓡ

— ESTD 1846 —
Dewar's®

DOUBLE AGED
· FOR EXTRA ·
SMOOTHNESS

WE AGE

WE BLEND

WE AGE AGAIN

LIVE TRUE

CHARTS

THE BIGGEST ARTISTS,
ALBUMS, AND SONGS
OF TODAY

Breaking Down a Month of Hits

A look at the top albums from the Rolling Stone Charts' first 30 days

Sheeran's Big Summer

Ed Sheeran hasn't scored a hit this year on par with 2017's ubiquitous "Shape of You," but that hardly hurt *No.6 Collaborations Project*, easily the most popular album of July. Sheeran's guest-heavy LP — featuring stars like Justin Bieber and Camila Cabello — amassed more than 200 million streams.

1

Ed Sheeran
No.6 Collaborations Project
Atlantic

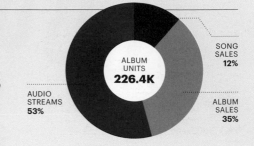

ALBUM UNITS **226.4K**

SONG SALES **12%**
AUDIO STREAMS **53%**
ALBUM SALES **35%**

SONG SALES **11%**
AUDIO STREAMS **87%**
ALBUM UNITS
ALBUM SALES **2%**

Lil Nas X Reigns

The success of Lil Nas X's *7* EP is driven almost entirely by just three songs: his breakout hit, "Old Town Road," which has topped the RS 100 for multiple weeks; "Panini," which interpolates Nirvana's "In Bloom"; and "Rodeo," which incorporates a typically boisterous verse from Cardi B.

The Biggest Baby

DaBaby's sharp, hammering raps have quickly become multiplatform hits. The North Carolina MC's "Suge" received more than 12,000 plays on the radio in a single week during July, while popular tracks like "Goin Baby" and "Baby Sitter" helped power *Baby on Baby* to more than 165 million streams in July.

	ALBUM UNITS
2 **Chris Brown** / **Indigo** / RCA	**205.9K**
3 **Billie Eilish** / **When We All Fall Asleep...** / Interscope	**189.3K**
4 **J. Cole, Dreamville** / **Revenge of the Dreamers III** / Interscope	**185.4K**
5 **Lil Nas X** / **7** / Columbia	**181.3K**
6 **Khalid** / **Free Spirit** / RCA	**116.4K**
7 **Mustard** / **Perfect Ten** / Interscope	**92.2K**
8 **DaBaby** / **Baby on Baby** / Interscope	**91.0K**
9 **Various Artists** / **Spider-Man: Into the Spider-Verse** / Interscope	**85.6K**
10 **Post Malone** / **Beerbongs & Bentleys** / Republic	**85.2K**

Pop's Can't-Miss Strategy: Call on Your Friends

The commercial benefits of collaboration have become abundantly clear in the streaming era: Packing albums with featured artists is a reliable way to bring in more listeners. Three of the 10 most popular albums in July followed this formula: Sheeran's *No.6 Collaborations Project*; *Revenge of the Dreamers III*, a showcase for J. Cole's Dreamville Records; and the soundtrack to *Spider-Man: Into the Spider-Verse*, featuring contributions from stars like Post Malone, Nicki Minaj, Juice Wrld, and Lil Wayne. Each collaborative album paired major names together to multiply its star power — and its streaming performance.

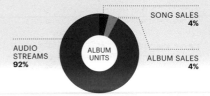

SONG SALES **4%**
AUDIO STREAMS **92%**
ALBUM UNITS
ALBUM SALES **4%**

Post Malone Is Forever

The music industry is increasingly focused on quick-rising viral hits, but Post Malone has a rarer quality: staying power. Fifteen months after he released *Beerbongs & Bentleys*, the album is still streaming at an impressive rate, even outstripping other huge releases like Drake's *Scorpion*, which came out several months after *Beerbongs & Bentleys*. Post's star-studded record, which features fellow chart-topping artists like Nicki Minaj and 21 Savage, broke Spotify records upon release and has barely lost momentum since.

○ SONG SALES
◉ AUDIO STREAMS
○ ALBUM SALES

This ranking compiles sales and streaming data from June 28th, 2019, to July 25th, 2019, as recorded by Alpha Data.

DaBaby

† ALBUM UNITS is a metric combining album sales, song sales, and audio streams, using a custom weighting system.

FROM TOP, LEFT TO RIGHT: PRINCE WILLIAMS/WIREIMAGE; 2: DEF JAM RECORDINGS; SCOTT DUDELSON/GETTY IMAGES; PARADIGM AGENCY; AUDIBLE TREATS

SPOTLIGHT

LIL KEED: HOW AN ATLANTA-RAP PHENOM FOUND HIS VOICE

ONE DAY LAST YEAR, Lil Keed's friends were pestering him to come to the parking lot of his apartment complex on Atlanta's Cleveland Avenue. One of the neighborhood's most popular exports, Young Thug, happened to be there, and the congregation knew this was their moment to showcase the neighborhood's rising star. "I had a song out called 'Bag,'" says Keed. "[My friends] kept playing it over and over again, and Thug was dancing to it. Thug finally walked up on me like, 'What you working on? Let me hear something.' So I let him hear some of my songs, and he's like, 'I got you.'"

FAST FACT

Young Thug isn't the only big rapper in Keed's corner — Drake is also a fan. "He texts me from time to time," Keed said.

Half a year later, Thug made good on his promise and signed Keed to his YSL Records imprint. Thug isn't just a mentor to Keed, he was a key influence, something felt through Keed's high-pitched yelp, chaotic ad-libs, and melody-driven verses. But on his new album, *Long Live Mexico*, the 21-year-old rapper branches out. Rapid bars are stacked next to tighter hooks, and the falsetto chirp transitions into something more mellow. This new approach allowed Keed to become the number-one artist on ROLLING STONE's Breakthrough 25, which measures the fastest-rising artists of the month. The spike was undoubtedly helped by the standout, woodwinds-heavy banger "Pull Up," featuring Lil Uzi Vert and YNW Melly.

Yet for all the album's jubilation, its title is a dedication to a friend Keed lost in early 2019. "Mexico was my brother," Keed shares. "He was going to be special, and he ended up dying....When he died, I changed the whole album up. I took the [album] picture by his gravesite." **CHARLES HOLMES**

Breakthrough Artists

The Rolling Stone Breakthrough 25 highlights the fastest-rising new artists

				UNIT GROWTH♦
1		**Lil Keed** 300		**8.3M**
2		**DaniLeigh** Def Jam		**6.2M**
3		**Fuerza Regida** Rancho Humilde		**5.4M**
4		**Quinn XCII** Columbia		**3.7M**
5		**Comethazine** Alamo		**3.1M**

♦ UNIT GROWTH refers to gains in audio streams over the previous month. Eligible artists must have released their debut in past five years. Chart covers growth from July 1st-31st.

Trending Songs

The Rolling Stone Trending 25 ranks the fastest-rising songs in the United States

				WEEKLY GROWTH‡
1		**Blueface** **Bussdown** Universal		**68%**
2		**Oliver Tree** **Alien Boy** Atlantic		**45%**
3		**Jeremy Zucker** **comethru** Republic		**44%**
4		**Stunna 4 Vegas** **Ashley** Interscope		**44%**
5		**Mabel** **Don't Call Me Up** Capitol		**32%**

‡ WEEKLY GROWTH refers to percentage growth in audio streams week over week. Eligible songs must have been released in the past three years. Chart covers the week of July 26th-August 1st.

To check out the full Rolling Stone Charts, read about our methodology, and more, visit RollingStone.com/Charts

Keed's Five Biggest Songs

Though Lil Keed's new album came out in June, his biggest song of July (as ranked by Song Units, a metric that combines sales and streams by a custom formula) was "Nameless," a hit from 2018.

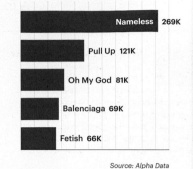

Nameless	269K
Pull Up	121K
Oh My God	81K
Balenciaga	69K
Fetish	66K

Source: Alpha Data

Rise of a Hip-Hop Hit

Take a look at the trajectory of "Bussdown," the hit from L.A. rapper Blueface, in audio streams, from its release to its rise to the top of the Trending Songs chart.

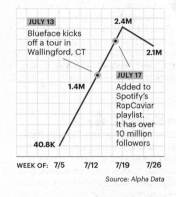

JULY 13 Blueface kicks off a tour in Wallingford, CT

2.4M

2.1M

1.4M

JULY 17 Added to Spotify's RapCaviar playlist. It has over 10 million followers

40.8K

WEEK OF: 7/5   7/12   7/19   7/26

Source: Alpha Data

2019's Most Streamed Artists

Drake is still the king of music streaming — for now, at least. Below are the top five artists of the year so far, ranked by **audio streams in billions.**

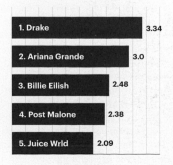

1. Drake	3.34
2. Ariana Grande	3.0
3. Billie Eilish	2.48
4. Post Malone	2.38
5. Juice Wrld	2.09

Source: Alpha Data

"IT WASN'T meant to be *Cavalcade of Stars*," says Sheryl Crow. "Hopefully it feels natural and cohesive." She's talking about her impressive mic-drop of a new album, *Threads*, which includes a Rock & Roll Hall of Fame induction ceremony's worth of guests (among them: Bonnie Raitt, Chuck D, Eric Clapton, Sting, Kris Kristofferson, St. Vincent, James Taylor, Maren Morris, Gary Clark Jr., Emmylou Harris, and Neil Young). The album is intended as the final full LP from Crow, 57, as she plans to focus on singles and other quicker releases. Still, she says, "Never say never."

This lineup is a real testament to how much your peers respect you. Is it also a bit of well-deserved muscle-flexing on your part?
My fear would be that anybody would think that. Honestly, I made a country record and promoted that, which felt like everything but having an authentic musical experience. So I wanted to just make music with people I love. And it did feel kind of like, "I don't know how to follow this up, and I don't really think I want to."

How important were Emmylou Harris and Stevie Nicks in helping you dream of a place for yourself in music?
Oh, my gosh, so important. Emmylou, she made so many records I loved even before she worked with Daniel Lanois, and then she went on to a whole new way of writing amazing stuff. *Red Dirt Girl* is a desert-island record for me. I hold her up as a great template. And Stevie is a fully realized artist. She looks at life as one big cinematic moment, and all her songs spring from that. And she still brings it live.

How did you pick "The Worst," an obscure country cut on *Voodoo Lounge,* for your Keith Richards duet?
The first time I heard that album, I was like, "I want to record that song." It's the quintessential pre-apology to a woman, like, "I'm not the kind of person you want

Q&A

Sheryl Crow

The singer-songwriter on her all-star new album, her future, and why Woodstock '99 was her worst live experience

By BRIAN HIATT

to get involved with." And I thought, "How great for a woman to sing that." Keith and I hung out for a couple of days in the studio – it's like being invited to the party.

You were in the audience at the '86 *Hail! Hail! Rock 'n' Roll* concert, where Steve Jordan, who produced this album, played with Richards and Chuck Berry, right?
I was a young schoolteacher in St. Louis, and I was there the first night. Cut to 30 years later, and I'm in the studio

with these two guys. To me, that's the American dream, that you can be a girl from a small town, and if you just keep putting one foot in front of the other, fantastical things can happen.

Two covers on this album — Bob Dylan's "Everything Is Broken," George Harrison's "Beware of Darkness" — really seem to speak to our present moment.
I am, for better or for worse, really suffering a great deal of sadness, and I cannot help it.

I'm raising two boys, and I'm sort of in mourning over what they are not going to get to experience. It's just a different world. Music is the place I go to when I can't seem to make any sense of it all. I get "Shut up and sing" all the time, so I'm shutting up and singing, and the songs I'm singing are speaking for me.

Where does your respect-your-elders ethos come from?
I know a lot of people that are like, "Hey, get off the plane,

it's time for someone else to take a ride." And I get that. But if people believe in old souls, I think I was born the way I am. Secondly, I grew up around parents who got off playing loud music as much as I do. Great music was always in my house.

You hesitated to add your vocals to Johnny Cash's, who covered your song "Redemption Day." Why?
I didn't want to tamper with it. Hearing him at the very beginning of it just grabbed me in such a deep and sobering way that I didn't want to put my voice on it. Johnny is untouchable. I had a big conversation with Steve [Jordan] – he's like, "Dude, you got to put your vocal on it, it's your record." I had to sing it a lot of times to figure out how to make it work.

Any guests you couldn't get?
I'm a huge Tom Petty fan, and if he were alive I'm sure I would've begged him to be a part of the album, although he probably would've declined. He wasn't really a guy who showed up on other people's records – unless you were a Wilbury, clearly.

Twenty years ago, you played Woodstock '99. What are your memories of that?
No one could bring in any food or water, and the bottled water was superexpensive. It bred rebellion. The porta-potty got turned over, and the next thing I know, I'm playing bass and there's feces being thrown on the bass rack right where I'm playing. Insane Clown Posse was right after us. It was the single worst gig I've ever been on. We got out of there as fast as we possibly could.

What do you think your post-album future will look like?
I mean, I'm certainly not saying I'm old, and I definitely feel like I still have some great songs in me. But I feel like it's almost a waste of time for me to have to wait for a whole album to put a song out, especially when I'm writing songs that I feel are bound by an immediacy. But I'm also finding my peace with not knowing what I'm going to do next. And that's good. ⟨R⟩

The Music, Politics and People
That Changed Our Culture

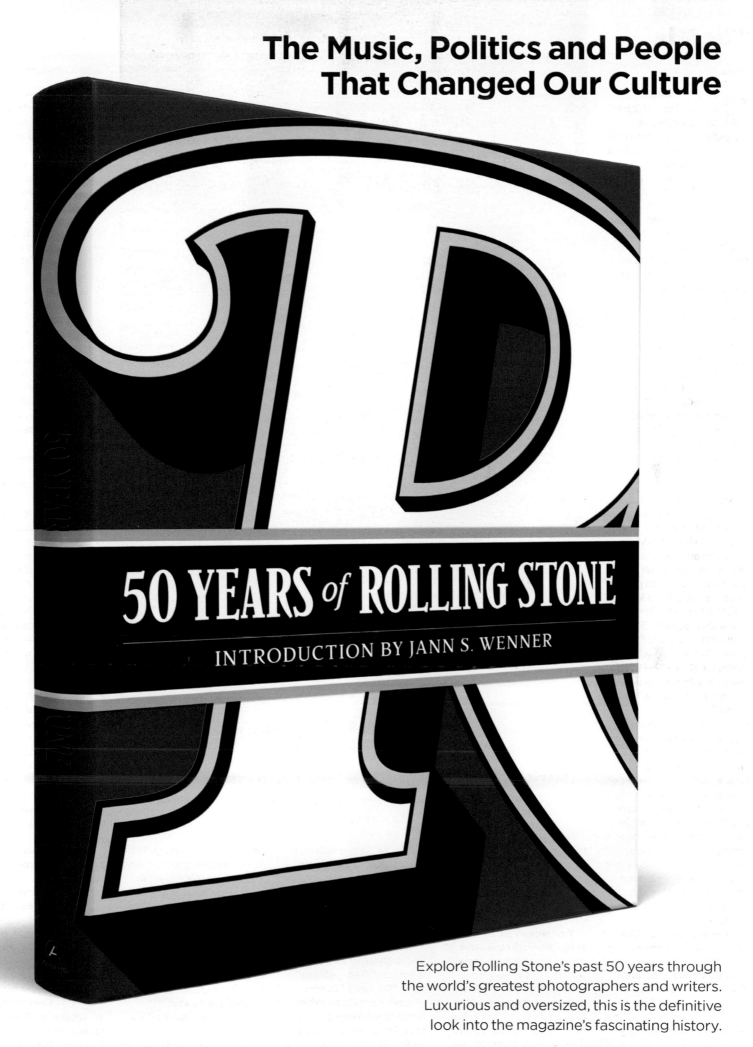

50 YEARS *of* ROLLING STONE

INTRODUCTION BY JANN S. WENNER

Explore Rolling Stone's past 50 years through the world's greatest photographers and writers. Luxurious and oversized, this is the definitive look into the magazine's fascinating history.

Random No

Cardi in Charge

Cardi B was in Los Angeles to appear on *Jimmy Kimmel*, where she and her husband, Offset, performed their new anti-clickbait single, "Clout." The couple just celebrated their daughter Kulture's first birthday. "I feel like I need a rest," she said. "But the happiness my baby brung me, I could do this over and over."

BEASTIES GET BACK
Ad-Rock and Mike D of the Beastie Boys were interviewed by LL Cool J at Beyond the Streets, a Brooklyn event that honored the 30th anniversary of their classic LP *Paul's Boutique*. "It's like a dope house party with an incredible DJ," said LL of the album.

WE'RE STILL STANDING
Pete Townshend and Julian Lennon hung out at a gala in Antibes, France, benefiting the Elton John AIDS Foundation. The next leg of Elton's farewell tour kicks off this month.

▶ **FOXX ROCKS**
Jamie Foxx, Woody Harrelson, apl.de.ap of the Black Eyed Peas, and Spike Lee partied it up in the Hamptons at a fundraiser for the Apollo Theater that took in more than $3 million. The night also saw performances by Pharrell Williams, Lenny Kravitz, Darlene Love, the Dave Matthews Band (who were joined onstage by Maggie Rogers), and the Isley Brothers, with the Roots serving as house band. The evening before the event, Foxx and will.i.am took over the DJ booth at a Southampton club and held it down for hours.

▲ **MAN OF THE GREENS** Justin Timberlake hit the links in Lake Tahoe, Nevada, at a celebrity golf outing, where he competed against superstar athletes like Steph Curry and Tony Romo and doled out high-fives to fans as he walked the fairways. A couple of weeks later, the singer headed into a New York studio to continue work on his next project. Earlier this year, he posted a photo of himself and longtime collaborator Timbaland on Instagram, adding "more claps that slap sooooooon come!"

▲ **FLIP IT UP** Australian indie-pop singer-songwriter G Flip turned in one of Lollapalooza's most talked-about sets by a new artist, playing songs off her debut LP, *About Us,* which intimately chronicles the ups and downs of a relationship. "Luckily, she didn't mind," G Flip (a.k.a. Georgia Flipo) said of the woman who inspired the songs on *About Us,* "otherwise, out of respect to her, this music would never have seen the light of day."

▲ **CHICAGO'S FINEST** A few days after releasing his new album, *The Big Day,* Chance the Rapper shared a prayer with fellow Windy City rapper Calboy. Calboy then joined Chance onstage at Lollapalooza for a powerful rendition of "No Problem," a track from the hip-hop superstar's 2016 album, *Coloring Book.* "That felt legendary, too, because I grew up listening to Chance since [his first mixtape] *10 Day,*" Calboy said of the performance. "It's a different type of feeling when you're onstage with him, after watching him onstage."

RANDOM QUOTE

"I've got so many parkas I can't hang them all up. I'd rather throw out the house than the parkas."

—Liam Gallagher

HELLO, DOLLY! Dolly Parton dueted with Brandi Carlile during a Newport Folk Festival set by an all-female collaborative that featured the Highwomen. "Dolly, I will always love you," Carlile said.

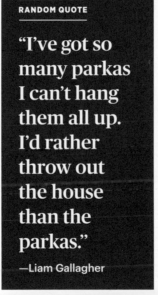

◀ **SHAQ JEEZEL**
Shaquille O'Neal appeared at Lollapalooza in his DJ Diesel guise, turning in an amped-up DJ set that featured smoke cannons, Queen samples, video screens showing video-game footage, huge plumes of pyro, and — when he played Kanye West's "Jesus Walks" — a visit from an actor dressed as the Messiah. At one point, Shaq even ventured into the mosh pit. "When I retired in 2011, I needed another adrenaline booster," he said. "No matter what you got going on in your life — stress, problems, whatever — there's two things that'll stop everything you're thinking about negatively: That's sports and music."

▲ **AMAZING MAGGIE** Self-proclaimed "witchy feminist rock star" Maggie Rogers had a busy Saturday at this year's Newport Folk Festival, playing solo on the main stage, then returning later that night to join Brandi Carlile and Sheryl Crow for a version of Crow's classic ballad "Strong Enough." "Thank you Sheryl Crow for this powerful anthem," Rogers tweeted after the show.

RS**ROAD**TEST

Three of music's hottest names introduce us to three of the year's coolest new rides. **PLUS** Updates on the latest in eco-friendly tech, the return of the VW Bus, and the race to build an all-electric pickup truck

Wystrach, Carson, and Duddy (from left)

MIDLAND

2020 JEEP GLADIATOR

Yes, the Gladiator looks like a Wrangler with a pickup bed bolted on the back — but underneath the sheet metal, there are some differences. A new rear suspension helps the Gladiator ride far smoother than Wranglers of old, which rattled change out of pockets even on the flattest suburban cul-de-sacs. The pickup's off-road cred is just as strong as Wrangler's, though its added length, about two and a half feet beyond the longest Wrangler, means the bed might scrape the ground coming off especially steep inclines. Fear not: Jeep installed protection under the rear bumper.

The Go-Anywhere Pickup

ESS CARSON, CAMERON DUDDY, and Mark Wystrach, a.k.a. Midland, are arguing about L.A. traffic. "You should take La Brea over to Sunset," Duddy, the band's bassist, says from the back seat of a fire-engine-red Jeep Gladiator Rubicon.

"No, not La Brea," says lead singer Wystrach, who's driving. "We want La Cienega – or, no, Crescent Heights."

All three guys currently call Austin home, but they used to live in L.A. So the drive up into the Hollywood Hills is also a trip down memory lane as they point out where friends lived, parties raged, and Wystrach nearly died in a motorcycle accident. The Gladiator's removable roof panels and doors are off – consider it a convertible that also happens to have a five-foot steel bed and a towing capacity of 7,000 pounds. "This truck would be pretty badass in Texas," Wystrach says.

A stop for lunch at the Laurel Canyon Country Store leads to talk of the band's new album, *Let It Roll*, which is informed by their growing pains over the past several years. The song "Playboys," for instance, touches on their early days touring: "Out here you get used to losing/Your friends, your lovers, and your mind."

"It's an autobiographical song about driving around in a pickup with our equipment in the bed – not even a tarp over it," Carson says. "The road is a beast that gets its claws in you and wants to keep you out there. It can be a seedy, dark existence." Today, though, the trio are all family men, and life on the road looks different. Carson is even selling some old pickup trucks to help pay for a tour bus, so his wife and kids can ride with him. "The biggest bummer would be that the three of us wouldn't be on the same bus," he says to his bandmates – then pauses. "Well, maybe I could still ride with you guys." KY HENDERSON

PHOTOGRAPH BY **Dan Prakopcyk**

The Faster, More Furious Sports Car

ITZ AND THE TANTRUMS owe their existence to an old station wagon. When frontman Michael Fitzpatrick was growing up in L.A., his father allowed only two kinds of music in the house: classical and opera. But when Fitz rode in his mom's car, he listened to Motown and soul on the radio. He liked the music so much he started singing along – and never stopped.

"Much to my parents' chagrin, by the time I was five or six years old, you couldn't shut me up," Fitz says while cruising on L.A.'s Angeles Crest Highway in Toyota's much-anticipated new Supra, a model that hasn't been sold in the U.S. since 1998. "Riding around listening to that music was the first place I could have my own musical identity, so it was completely tied in with car culture."

Fitz admits he's gotten more than his fair share of speeding tickets – then floors the Supra's gas pedal. The 3.0-liter, 335-horsepower turbocharged engine launches the car down the mountain road, while precise handling prevents it from launching *off* the road.

"It's been a hot minute since I've driven in a legit sports car," says the father of three young boys, whose daily driver is an SUV. "It's kind of awesome."

Lack of sports cars notwithstanding, Fitz has spent plenty of time on the road lately. He says a decade's worth of relentless touring, which put literal and figurative distance between him and his friends and family, contributed to the feelings of confusion and depression he faced while writing songs for the band's new album, *All the Feels*. The 17-song record features plenty of the party anthems for which they're famous, but it also has contemplative and even sad songs – though, because it's Fitz and the Tantrums, several are still extremely danceable. Fitz says he's more proud of this album than any other. "That cheesy fucking adage is so true," he says. "It's not the destination, it's the journey." K.H.

2020 TOYOTA SUPRA

Fans of classic Japanese sports cars, nitrous boosts, and *The Fast and the Furious* antihero Dominic Toretto — i.e., the many car buffs who worship the Supra Mk4 made in the 1990s — will notice that the muscular rumble of this Supra's engine sounds more German than Japanese. That's because Toyota sourced the motor, along with the eight-speed transmission and chassis for this limited-production model, from BMW, to keep manufacturing costs down.

THE YEAR'S BEST CAR STEREOS

Smaller and more plentiful speakers, better sound isolation, and reactive mood lighting are revolutionizing the car-audio game

2020 Kia Soul GT
Harman Kardon Sound System

▶ This boxy, fun-and-gun crossover is a jolt to drive, but it really overdelivers in the entertainment department, thanks to an available 10-speaker, 640-watt system featuring a subwoofer solid enough to draw eyes at intersections. Bonus: After dark, you can select an array of mood-lighting scenarios to enhance your listening experience, including a few that make the speaker-surrounding LEDs pulse to the beat of the music. That may sound slightly corny, but in practice it's pretty trippy and actually cool. **FROM $20,290** *kia.com*

2020 Lincoln Aviator
Revel Ultima 3D Audio System

▶ Most vehicles notify you that you left your lights on with a low-fi ding; this new, three-row SUV does it in dramatic fashion with the help of the Detroit Symphony Orchestra, which recorded six different alert chimes to ring out in a variety of scenarios. Laminated glass on the windshield and side panels and extensive underbody insulation serve to make the cabin library-quiet should you need some peace. But if you don't, a 28-speaker sound system kicks out the jams with sparkling fidelity. **FROM $51,100** *lincoln.com*

2020 Acura RDX
ELS Studio 3D Premier Audio System

▶ Foo Fighters producer Elliot Scheiner turned this two-row crossover into a rolling listening room with an obsessively tuned sound system that features 16 speakers, including four tiny units embedded in the ceiling, one above each passenger's head. Those top-firing speakers add a 3D height effect and eliminate sonic obstructions like headrests, so each rider gets front-row sound. Plus, they enable you to better direct which seats get the brunt of the system's volume. **$43,800** *acura.com* JESSE WILL

INSIDE THE VEGAN CAR

WHEN IT COMES TO INTERIORS, THE DEFINITION OF LUXURY IS NO LONGER LEATHER

WHILE THE RICH SMELL of leather has been a hallmark of high-end cars for decades, socially conscious buyers are changing that. You can now order a Range Rover Velar or Evoque (left) with a vegan interior featuring fabrics made from eucalyptus and even recycled plastic bottles. Early next year, Volvo will launch its plug-in Polestar 2 sedan with vegan seats, and Tesla will soon offer its Model 3 and Model Y free of animal products. Even mass brands like Ford are experimenting with soybean-based foams and materials derived from algae oil. The trend is near a "tipping point," says Land Rover design director Gerry McGovern. "Leather seats are a bit old-fashioned." J.W.

AN ALL-TIME LEGEND KEEPS ON TRUCKIN'
VW IS REVIVING THE TYPE 2 BUS — AND NOW IT'S BATTERY-POWERED

LONG BEFORE #VANLIFE was a thing and Jerry Garcia played his first guitar, the Volkswagen microbus rolled off German assembly lines in 1950. Roomy enough to pack with surfboards, camping gear, or festival-going flower children, it became an icon of the counterculture movement before disappearing from U.S. showrooms in 1979. But now, the VW Bus is roaring back — silently. In 2022, Volkswagen plans to begin producing a plug-in electric model, based on the I.D. Buzz concept vehicle shown here, which mimics the original van's monolithic, overhang-free look and boasts tech upgrades including wraparound ambient LED lighting, and near-autonomous driving features. A huge battery will provide enough juice for the Bus to travel up to 300 miles on a single charge, and it will take an 80 percent charge in a half hour via a DC fast charger (you'll need to map out those stations before hitting the road to trail Phish). Unlike the anemic models of the past, which made highway on-ramps harrowing, the plug-in Bus will produce 369 horsepower — that's more than 15 times that of the OG van, more akin to a muscle car. And the electric powertrain will enable not just a "frunk," or front trunk, as in the Fifties-era models (which housed an engine in the back), but plenty of interior flexibility. Since the I.D. Buzz's battery hides in the floor and the two electric motors sit at the axles, the cabin space above is rife with possibilities: The concept vehicle features seats that can be moved around on rails to face each other, turn into tables, or fold flat. It's more like a living room than a car. "We want to guarantee that you can sleep in it," says Klaus Bischoff, Volkswagen's chief designer, who drove and camped in a clas-

sic Bus during high school. "The Type 2 moved a generation and became a part of music and pop culture. We had that in mind — striving to build something soulful. This technology will help us realize that." Pricing hasn't been announced, but VW has stated that it won't stray far from similar, conventionally powered vehicles. Some analysts have speculated it will start around $50,000. J.W.

HAYLEY KIYOKO

The All-Electric SUV

AYLEY KIYOKO KNOWS CARS. Her dream rides have included a Bugatti Veyron – among the fastest production cars on Earth – and classics like a '57 Chevy and an Austin-Healey. She can talk everything from torque curves to five-star safety ratings. "I'm obsessed," Kiyoko says as she pilots an Audi e-tron through the tree-lined streets of L.A.'s ritzy Bel Air neighborhood. "My dad used to keep auto magazines in the bathroom to browse, and we went to car shows for Father's Day every year. Cars are my steez."

Driving with music, on the other hand, is not. In her own car – an Audi Q5 – Kiyoko prefers listening to nothing at all. "I like driving in silence because it's the only time I can collect my thoughts," says the singer-songwriter crowned "Lesbian Jesus" by her fans. "Sometimes I'll get home and just sit in my car for a while. It's a safe space where no one can bother me. But it makes my friends nuts – after 30 minutes of driving they'll be like, 'Uh, can you turn on some music?' "

The roomy e-tron is a great pick for anyone who loves silence. The SUV, Audi's first all-electric vehicle, offers a drive free of engine noise and road racket. And there's still plenty of juice in the tank as Kiyoko swings south toward Beverly Hills, talking about the future. She's working on an album she describes as "more daring and evolved" than her previous work – it will include her latest single, "I Wish," a midtempo lament about a callous lover – and while her online popularity and status in the LGBTQ community mean the world to her, Kiyoko hopes for some old-school accolades. "I want a platinum record!" she says. "That, to me, is a measure of mainstream success. Plus being played on the radio." Which would be a pretty good reason to finally listen to music in her car. KY HENDERSON

2020 AUDI E-TRON

While its listed range of 204 miles per charge is lower than that of some competitors, Audi touts the e-tron's ability to gain 80 percent of its charge in 30 minutes and a full charge in 45 when using a 150-kilowatt-capable station. Starting at $74,800, the car features a Bang & Olufsen sound system and optional "air quality package" that ionizes the cabin and emits fragrance.

TRUCKS TAKE CHARGE
MAKE WAY FOR A NEW BREED OF ECO-FRIENDLY PICKUPS

IN THE WORLD of pickup trucks, tradition reigns and Western tropes abound. You can walk into a Ram dealership and get a dashboard that's been cattle-branded, after all. But change is coming, fast. A wave of emission-free, plug-in pickups is on the way, and you won't need cowboy boots to drive them. In March, when TESLA held a webcast to unveil its compact crossover, the Model Y, a surprise teaser image appeared: the glowing silhouette of a truck bed. CEO Elon Musk later confirmed it showed his "cyberpunk" vision of an electric pickup now in development. Musk has said the company is aiming to build a truck that's more work-capable than a Ford F-150 and a better sports car than a Porsche 911. No small feat. But he's not the only one with such lofty goals. Even further along is the Detroit-based outfit truck will boast a range of 400 miles and a zero-to-60-mph time of three seconds, in addition to functional features like a pass-through "gear tunnel" behind the back seats that easily holds surfboards or skis. As with the Tesla pickup, the idea is to seduce buyers who wouldn't otherwise consider a truck. "We feel that we're speaking to a lot of people outside of the traditional truck buyer — the R1T will have efficiency and refinement that's just currently not available," says Rivian creative director Larry Parker. "These people will be coming out of Land Rovers and things of that nature." Another startup, BOLLINGER, is now accepting reservations for its retro, rugged, Detroit-built plug-in B2 pickup, a boxy workhorse with a 5,000-pound payload. And the big boys are getting involved, too: Chevy is developing a plug-in version of its full-size

Rivian's sleek R1T (top) will haul huge payloads and ford three feet of water. The Bollinger B2 (above) has removable rear seats.

RIVIAN. Using $1.2 billion in funding from Amazon and Ford, the company plans to produce its rugged yet refined R1T model by 2020 at a former Mitsubishi plant in Normal, Illinois. The $69,000 Silverado, and Ford is working on an electric F-150. The company recently released a video of a prototype towing a train weighing more than a million pounds — no cattle or lassos in sight. J.W.

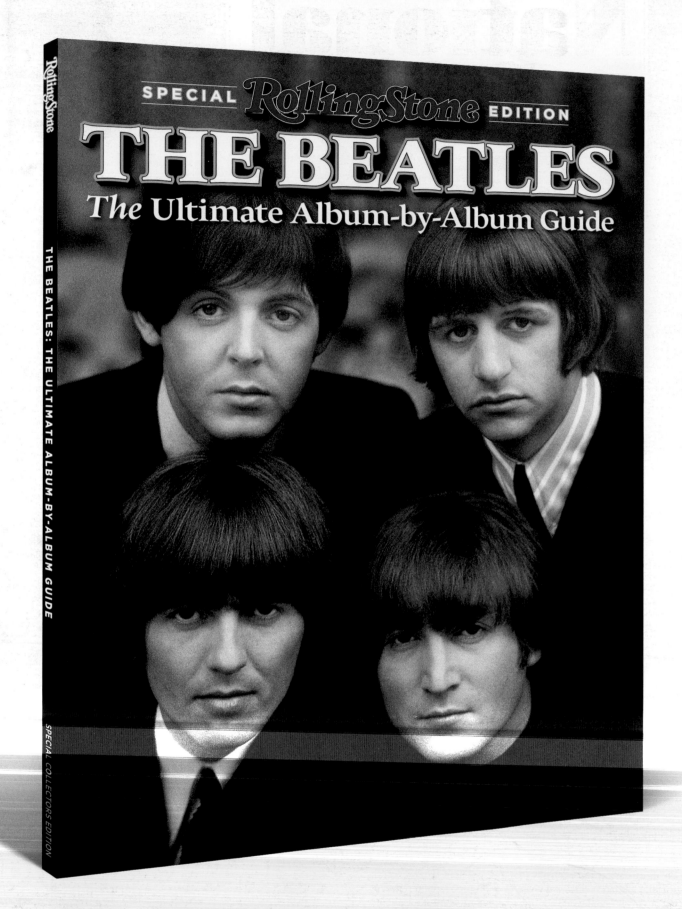

Trump 2020: Be Very Afraid

America is the first country to ever elect a Mad King, and the way things are going, we may be dumb enough to do it twice

By MATT TAIBBI

ARLY EVENING, August, Cincinnati, Ohio. The Queen City's many bridges are sealed off, its sky is dirty with helicopters, and seemingly every cop for 100 miles is patrolling Pete Rose Way along the Ohio River. A crowd of 20,000 or more stands in punishing heat, waiting to enter U.S. Bank Arena. The evil rumor buzzing down the line of MAGA hats is that not everyone will get in to see Donald Trump.

"Can we just get in for a minute?" complains a boy of about 10 to his mother. There are a lot of kids here.

Donald Trump doesn't visit Middle America. He descends upon it. His rallies are awesome spectacles. Gawkers come down from the hills. If NASA traveled the country holding showings of the first captured alien life-form, the turnout would be similar. The pope driving monster trucks might get this much attention.

Almost everyone in line is wearing 45 merch. Trump is the most T-shirtable president in history, and it's not even close. Trumpinator tees are big (2020: I'LL BE BACK), but you'll also see Trump as Rambo (complete with headband, ammo belt, and phallic rocket-launcher), Trump as the Punisher (a Trump pompadour atop the famous skull), even Trump as Superman (pulling his suit open to reveal a giant T).

Slogans include TRUMP 2020: GRAB 'EM BY THE PUSSY AGAIN! and the ubiquitous TRUMP 2020: FUCK YOUR FEELINGS.

One merch hawker – an African American man with a visor, wraparound sunglasses, and spiked, dyed-white hair – is snaking through the crowd, pushing a T-shirt: DONALD FUCKIN' TRUMP. On the back, the shirt reads BITCH I'M THE PRESIDENT! "Five bucks for hats, 10 for tees!" he yells. "Bitch, I'm the president! Make America great again!"

"Four more years!" someone in the crowd yells back, to cheers.

Two and a half years into his presidency, Trump has already staked a claim to a role in history usually reserved for hereditary monarchs at the end of a line of inbreeding. Historians will list him somewhere between Vlad the Impaler and France's Charles VI, who thought his buttocks were made of glass.

Much of America loves its Mad King, whose works are regularly on display. Russians under Ivan the Terrible used to watch dogs being hurled over the Kremlin walls when the tsar's mood was bad. Americans have grown used to late-night insults tweeted at nuclear powers from the White House bedroom.

Royal lunacy is traditionally a secret, but in Twitter-age America it's a shared national experience. We are all somersaulting down and out the sanity chute. The astonishing thing about Trump is that he wasn't foisted on us by a council of Bourbons, or by succession law. We elected the man, and are poised to do it again.

History will judge us harshly for this, and will look with particular venom at Trump's political opponents in both parties, who over the years were unable to win popularity contests against a man most people would not leave alone with a decent wristwatch, let alone their children.

Trump's original destiny was the destruction of the Republicans as a viable entity in modern American politics. Then he ran a general election like he was trying to lose, and won. Now his legacy is the spectacular end of America's fragile racial consensus.

Ten years ago, an African American won the White House in a landslide; today, the president is somewhere between a Klansman and Jimmy the Greek. The media legend is that Trump succeeds because he's a racist, but this undersells it. Trump is 50 years behind the worst elements of the Republican Party, which spent decades carefully stuffing race under bromides like "states' rights" and "free stuff." The GOP now is in an all-out bucket brigade to rescue the dog whistle.

The rescue is failing. We've gone from Trump being skeptical of Obama's citizenship to musing about "very fine" neo-Nazis to a Twitter version of "Go back to Africa." In Cincinnati, even his most hardcore supporters talk about wanting him to shut up. "I wish," says one fan, "he would edit himself a little bit."

For all this, every time Trump seems headed for the dustbin of history, he bounces up again off the messageless paralysis of his Democratic opposition. When Trump vanquished a giant primary field of Republicans in 2016, Democrats cheered. When they lost the general election, they acted like it was an unrelated surprise event, an outrage to decency itself. They remain ineffective as anything but a punchline to the Trump story.

This cycle has led to more alienation and made the 2020 election a gruesome, exhausting black comedy. This is our penance for turning the presidential campaign into a bread-and-circus entertainment. Middle Americans got so used to getting nothing out of elections, they started treating national politics for what it had become to them, a distant, pretentious sitcom.

Now they're writing their own script. They can't arrange for Jake Tapper to be fed to a shark, so they'll settle for rolling Donald Trump into Washington. It's hard to see right now, it being the end of our society and all, but the situation is not without humor, in a "What does this button marked DETONATE do?" sort of way. Can America shoot itself in the head a second time? It sounds, appropriately enough, like the premise of a Trump TV show.

ERE'S HOW degraded the political landscape has become: Mike Pence looks like a vice president now. In 2016, especially after the "grab 'em by the pussy" episode, the genuflecting Indianan often came across like a man appointed public defender to a ring of child cannibals. Now, onstage in Cincinnati, he looks stoked to be introducing His Trumpness.

"And now, it's my high honor and distinct privilege to introduce you to my friend" – Pence sells it hard – "and the 45th president

READERS' POLL

Do you believe that impeaching Trump would hurt Democrats' chances in 2020?

27%
Yes

73%
No

Go to Rolling Stone.com for next issue's poll.

TIMELINE — THE LONG VIEW: MITCH MCCONNELL — THE GREAT OBSTRUCTIONIST

OCT. 2010 | APRIL 2013 | NOV. | NOV. | MARCH 2016 | SEPT. | NOV.

A REAL PATRIOT
McConnell says his top priority as Senate minority leader is making Barack Obama a "one-term president."

NO GUN CONTROL
In the wake of Sandy Hook, McConnell filibusters to block bipartisan **gun-control** measures that would expand background checks and ban assault weapons.

JUDICIAL SABOTAGE
McConnell leads a successful effort to block 79 **Obama nominees**, compared to 68 blocked under all other presidents combined since 1967.

REAL THREAT
"You'll regret this," McConnell warns when the Dems **abolish the rule** requiring a 60-vote majority for lower-court nominations, to overcome GOP obstruction.

SUPREME COURT OUTRAGE
Now majority leader, McConnell blocks Supreme Court nominee **Merrick Garland**, refusing even to hold hearings, arguing, with no basis in the Constitution, Obama did not have the right in an election year. "One of my proudest moments," said McConnell.

COUNTRY FIRST?
McConnell questions CIA report on **Russian election interference** and threatens political retaliation if Obama releases the findings before the election.

VOTER MOTIVATION
Twenty-six percent of **Trump voters** say filling the Supreme Court seat McConnell managed to hold open was the most important factor in why they voted for Trump.

of the United States of America, President Donald Trump!"

The crowd bursts into roars, hoots, cheers. Trump pops out onstage. Lee Greenwood's "God Bless the USA" booms over the stadium.

Trump takes his sweet time to get to the podium. He gives photogs every pose: the clap, the wave, the arms akimbo, the blown kiss. It's "I'm Too Sexy" brought to politics. A lot of candidates scan crowds like they're looking for the sniper, but Trump acts like he's ready for a mass frottage session.

"There's that, too," agrees a young Trump supporter named Andrew Walls later. "He l-o-o-o-ves what he does."

Trump gives a double-fist pump in the direction of a man in a red headband and a green army vest. When Trump looks in his direction, the man spasms like a dog blowing a load. Others are waving their arms like Pentecostals or doing V-for-victory signs. It's pandemonium.

Trump takes the lectern. His hair has visibly yellowed since 2016. It's an amazing, unnatural color, like he was electrocuted in French's mustard. His neckless physique is likewise a wonder. He looks like he ate Nancy Pelosi.

"You know," Trump says, referencing the Democrats' debate in Detroit, "I was watching the so-called debates last night...."

Booo!

"...That was long, long television."

That part is true enough. One wonders if Trump scheduled a rally the day after the debates on purpose, to steal the end of the flailing Democrats' news cycle. He goes on:

"The Democrats spent more time attacking Barack Obama than they did attacking me, practically," he says, to cheers. "And this morning that's all the fake news was talking about."

TRUMP MERCH
A superfan of the 45th president at the August rally in Cincinnati. Popular items at events include Trumpinator tees ("2020: I'll Be Back"), Trump as Rambo (with headband and rocket-launcher), and the ever-present slogan, "Trump 2020: Fuck Your Feelings."

BOOOOOOO!!!!

Nobody draws bigger catcalls than the "fake" news media. Trump knows this and pauses to let the bile rise. He expresses pleasure at being back in "the American heart land," which he pronounces as if he's just learned the term.

He then reflects on his 2016 run, when hordes of people turned out to send him to D.C., from places he, Trump, would never have visited, except maybe by plane crash.

"You came from the mountains and the valleys and the rivers, and, uh, you came for –" He seems to not know what comes after rivers. "I mean, look, you came from wherever you came from, and there were a lot of you."

He ends up telling a story about early voting in Tennessee in 2016, and a congressman who told him if the whole country was voting like this, he was going to win by a lot. "And we won," he says. "And we won by a lot."

Press accounts will call this a lie, and of course it is, and even the crowd knows it. But they cheer anyway. In response, Trump stops and does his trademark stump flourish, turn-

ing sideways to flash his iguanoid profile before stalking around the lectern in resplendent, obese glory, inviting all to *Get a load of me!*

It's indulgent, absurd, narcissistic, and appalling, unless you're a Trump fan, in which case it's hilarious, a continuation of the belly laughs that began in many parts of America with Hillary Clinton's concession speech.

Trump crowds have changed. At the beginning of 2016, trying to pull quotes out of Trump rallies was like stopping a bunch of straight men who'd just whacked each other off behind a trailer. They didn't want to talk about it.

As time progressed, the crowd's profile widened. You met union members, veterans, and where it got weird was the stream of people who appeared to be neither traditional Republicans nor, seemingly, interested in politics at all. Among both young and old, people turned out who had no conception of Trump as anything but a TV star. This second group's numbers seemed to have swelled.

"I watched the *Celebrity Apprentice,* and I loved that," says Jackie Hoffman, a 60-year-old grandmother who gushes "we never had" someone like Trump run for president before. "Ronald Reagan was a celebrity, but he wasn't, like, a big celebrity," she says.

"I just want to get a feel for the spectacle," says Walls. As we talk, he's gazing at a stand full of Trump merch. He likes the Punisher motif, but also the Terminator tee. "If I had money," he says, "I'd probably buy that."

Walls and his friend James Monroe drove in from Kentucky. Walls is an enthusiastic Trump supporter, Monroe not – he's here for the show. Though they disagree about Trump's politics, they express surprise he won the last time.

This is a common theme, when you ask people what impresses them most about Trump, i.e., that he won despite the press. The news media rate somewhere between herpes and ISIS in much of the country. "A lot of the media are very liberal," says Monroe. "I don't know how he won."

APRIL 2017 | **JULY** | **DEC.** | **OCT. 2018** | **JAN. 2019** | **APRIL** | **MAY**

GOING NUCLEAR
McConnell uses "nuclear option," abolishing filibuster for Supreme Court nominations, to ram through Trump nominee **Neil Gorsuch** with a simple majority vote.

'SKINNY REPEAL'
McConnell tries to repeal Obamacare, holds no public hearings on bill that would strip 16 million of health insurance, but is foiled by **John McCain**'s thumbs-down.

DEFICIT HYPOCRISY
McConnell leads the passage of the **Trump tax bill** that benefits corporations and the wealthy, and will raise the deficit by $1.4 trillion. When the deficit does indeed balloon the next year, McConnell blames Medicare and other social safety nets.

NUCLEAR SEQUEL
McConnell's Senate-rules revamp pays off again as **Brett Kavanaugh** is confirmed to the Supreme Court through a simple majority vote.

UN-DEMOCRATIC
McConnell calls Dem legislation to increase voter turnout by making **Election Day** a holiday a "power grab."

BY ANY MEANS
Further **dismantling procedural rules**, McConnell decreases Senate debate time for lower-level Trump nominees from 30 hours to two hours.

NEW HEIGHTS OF HYPOCRISY
When asked what he'd do if a **Supreme Court** vacancy arose in 2020 before the election, McConnell grins: "Oh, we'd fill it."

Skylar Easter, 23, and Sahara Hollingshead, 19, are a young couple who came down from Circleville, Ohio. Skylar's got long blond hair, a beard, and tie-dye shirt, and looks vaguely like the *True Romance* version of Brad Pitt. Sahara's got purple glasses and says, "There are more minorities and women employed right now than there's been in almost 30 years. That's great." Both recently landed jobs at a company called TriMold, making parts for Hondas. "We stand in one place and operate a machine," says Skylar. Sahara likes Trump's attitude, because he's "not scared to go for it."

The most common remark you hear from Trump voters is that he's "relatable" and isn't "phony." Blue-state audiences tempted to howl at this should try to understand this phenomenon, because it speaks to a legitimate problem Democrats have.

The average American likes meat, sports, money, porn, cars, cartoons, and shopping. Less popular: socialism, privilege-checking, and the world ending in 10 years. Ironically, perhaps because of Trump, Democratic Party rhetoric in 2020 is relentlessly negative about the American experience. Every speech is a horror story about synagogue massacres or people dying without insulin or atrocities at the border. Republicans who used to complain about liberals "apologizing for America" were being silly, but 2020 Democrats sound like escapees from the Killing Fields.

Ronald Reagan once took working-class voters away from Democrats by offering permission to be proud of the flag. Trump offers permission to occupy the statistical American mean: out of shape, suffering from gas, poorly read, anti-intellectual, treasuring things above meaning, and hiding an awful credit history.

Trump in this way is more all-American than Mark Spitz, Liberace, Oprah, Audie Murphy, and Marilyn Monroe. He's a monument to the consumption economy. He represents fake boobs, the short con, the tall tale, gas guzzlers, and a hundred other American traditions.

This is why the endless chronicling of Trump's lies does little to dent his popularity. Trump's voters don't need to read Politi-Fact to see what Trump's about. They see it in his waistline. Few politicians in history have revealed what they are to voters more than Trump. Christ, we even know what the man's penis looks like.

"The cool thing about Trump," says 38-year-old Cincinnati native Jeremy Holtkamp, "is that it's just about being an American."

TRUMP'S POLITICAL STRATEGY is primitive but effective. He picks something that polls badly, and kicks it in the crotch. Then he backs off and lets three eternal truths do the rest of the work.

One: A news media that pretends moral outrage will greedily cover his every move (cable-news profits have soared 36 percent since Trump began his run four years ago).

Two: In a fractured political landscape, the so-called "legitimate" politicians who are his main competition will spend more time fighting each other than him. This is because intellectuals can't bring themselves to take Trump's dumbed-down version of politics seriously.

Third: America's upper classes and their proxies in government and media have no capacity for self-reflection, and will make asses of themselves in a fight. This is where Trump makes his living, getting people who should know better to rise to his bait. It's a simple formula: Incite brawls that seem like clear political losers, only to eventually maneuver controversies to his advantage.

Trump launched his 2020 re-election campaign on June 18th in Orlando. Within a month, he was picking his first major campaign fight. The backdrop was Trump's decision to increase the number of criminal prosecutions for illegal border entry. His innovation was making systematic the separation of families in custody, a move that seemed to have no practical purpose except as a deterrent of the *Game of Thrones* heads-on-spikes variety.

When everyone from the American Academy of Pediatrics to his wife to Lindsey Graham expressed revulsion – dude, kids? – Trump finally signed an executive order reversing the policy. He then characteristically blamed the mess on Democrats. By then the situation had become a fiasco and, like all things in the Trump era, a media goat rope of monstrous proportions.

In response, House Speaker Nancy Pelosi and her "mighty moderates" attempted to pass a bipartisan border bill backed by Senate Majority Leader Mitch McConnell. Progressives who have called for the entire border-enforcement machinery to be reformed freaked.

A representative from Wisconsin compared Democratic moderates to child abusers, and debonair Twitter subversive Alexandria Ocasio-Cortez cried, "Hell, no." When Pelosi yawned back at Ocasio-Cortez and three other young female members for "their public whatever and their Twitter world," the Bronx congresswoman called Pelosi out for the "singling out of newly elected women of color."

In perhaps the most predictable moment of his presidency, a gleeful Trump jumped on this Democrat-on-Democrat racial food fight. Using the backdrop of Marine One, he said Ocasio-Cortez was being "very disrespectful," adding, "I don't think Nancy can let that go on."

Nancy! The lascivious familiarity with which Trump dropped her name must have stuck like a tongue in Pelosi's ear. The speaker, from that moment, was cornered. A step forward meant welcoming the boils-and-all embrace of Donald Trump. A step back meant bitter intramural surrender and a likely trip to intersectionality re-education camp.

A normal, self-aware politician, meaning one who is not Donald Trump, would have waited for Pelosi to step off this land mine. But Trump then issued his infamous tweet about "the squad" – Reps. Ocasio-Cortez, Ilhan Omar, Rashida Tliab, and Ayanna Pressley – needing to "go back and help fix the totally broken and crime infested places from which they came."

For the 10 millionth time since he launched his presidential campaign, Trump seemed to

TRUMP'S POLL NUMBERS

According to a recent Gallup poll, Trump's approval rating is at 42 percent. Among voters over 50, he rises to 49 percent, and with white voters he climbs to 53 percent approval. Eighty-nine percent of Republicans support the president, as do 38 percent of independents. Trump struggles with educated voters: 41 percent with four years of college and just 33 percent with post-grad experience back him. More worrying for Dems, his ratings are similar to Obama's before 2012.

make a fatal miscalculation, revealing himself to be a meandering, incoherent racist on a political suicide mission. But we should recognize by now, these outbursts by Trump are never fatal.

The practical impact of Trump's summer freakouts was to make everyone on Earth forget the original controversy. Instead, the country ended up engaged in a full-scale melee over Pelosi's racial attitudes, the relative dirtiness of Baltimore, whether or not Al Sharpton hates white people, and a dozen other questions.

Soon, the Democratic candidates were in such a fury about all things immigration that they ganged up on hapless Joe Biden for not stopping the "Deporter-in-Chief," Obama.

This was classic Trump. He creates controversies so quickly that no one can keep track of them all. When the dust settles, everyone is covered with welts and King Donald is bragging about having done it all on purpose, which he may have. In the end, what everyone remembers is Trump antagonists tying themselves in knots over his whims.

AMERICA IS MESSED UP, sure, but are we *this* messed up? What if we didn't have a perma-tweeting Archie Bunker president, or turned off our TVs? Trump's 2016 victory only happened with a slew of unwitting accomplices. Republicans split the primary vote, Democrats nominated a high-negatives insider, and the media not only tossed to Trump billions of dollars in free coverage, but also constantly validated his mockery with snooty mis-predictions. A child knows not to fall for the pull-my-finger joke a second time. But the assembled brainpower of institutional America seems determined to clear a path for Trump by playing straight man again.

Back on Pete Rose Way, a meager crowd of 100 or so protesters remains gathered across the street. A few anguished-looking college-educated types hold a banner reading "Hate Has No Home Here." Walking up and down their side is a young activist with a bullhorn.

"I hate to break the bad news to you," he shouts across the asphalt divide. "Trump doesn't give a shit about working people!"

"Fuck you!" one of a trio of young MAGA dudes shouts in reply.

His buddies are laughing and high fiving. They're having a blast. The anguish of the lefty protesters is the best part.

Throughout Trump's speech, spectators came down to taunt the libs. It got tense enough that a row of helmeted cops showed up, stringing patrol bicycles end to end in the middle of the street to create an ad-hoc barricade.

"He's a fucking con man," the would-be Ortega on the other side is chanting now. "Don the con...All power to the working class!"

"We are the working class, buddy!" an older man shouts. More laughs.

"No more hate!" the protesters chant.

"Four more years, bitch!" comes the reply.

The road is only four lanes wide, but it might as well be a continent. Two groups of people, calling each other assholes across a barricade. Welcome to America in the Donald Trump era. **Ⓡ**

Why Can't California Solve Its Housing Crisis?

It's the epicenter of the tech industry and the wealthiest, most progressive state in the union, but homelessness is surging – and no one can agree on how to fix it

By TESSA STUART

WHEN THE SHIMMERING, state-of-the-art, $1.3 billion Levi's Stadium opened its doors in Santa Clara, it was hailed as the pinnacle of technological innovation. Concessions delivered to your seat at the touch of a button! Bluetooth beacons to navigate you with pinpoint precision! High-speed internet throughout! And to top it all off, not a single public cent was spent. The whole thing was privately financed, partly through seat licenses sold to fans at prices ranging from $2,000 to $250,000 – a testament to the exorbitant, almost incomprehensible wealth generated in the greater Bay Area in recent decades, and a gambit that happened to price out a huge swath of 49ers faithful.

Adelle Amador has been a Niners fan since she was a kid living on the east side of San Jose. Her husband, Maurice, is a supervisor at one of the stadium's club-level restaurants. "He's been working there since they cut the ribbon," she says. The stadium opened five years ago. The couple and their children, ages three to 14, have been homeless for about the same amount of time. Adelle works too, as a cashier, but the

ON THE STREETS
The city of San Jose opened a safe parking lot where 17 homeless families can sleep in their cars. "It's not a solution," says one housing advocate. "We're not ending homelessness that way."

couple's combined income is not enough to afford a market-rate apartment in the city where they've spent their entire lives.

They've stayed with friends and family, cycled through shelters, motels, and garages, slept at drive-in movie theaters, and parked their Ford Explorer near Coyote Creek, a homeless encampment San Jose has been trying to eradicate for years, where Adelle and her husband would trade shifts sleeping. "We've been where there's people trying to open the handles to your car door," Amador says. Most nights, "My main thing was just, 'Oh, God, just please get us to the morning, please, God.'"

Last December, the family began spending nights in the parking lot of a community center in a residential neighborhood just off the Capitol Expressway, about 30 minutes, give or take, from the headquarters of some of the country's richest companies – Apple's Infinite Loop, in Cupertino; the Googleplex, in Mountain View; and Facebook, in Menlo Park. On those manicured campuses, employees are generating billions of dollars shaping every aspect of our futures, but just outside, the lower-wage workers who make this community run are strug-

gling to meet a basic human need: shelter. Google recently pledged $1 billion to help ease the Bay Area's housing crunch – but that sum is only eye-popping until you hear experts explain it would cost $14 billion to execute the company's vision of building 20,000 homes. Google's is a well-intentioned gesture, but one that illustrates how the problem facing the Bay Area, and California at large, is much worse than even its brightest minds can comprehend.

The city of San Jose opened the parking lot to homeless families after fielding hundreds of complaints from locals confounded by the increasing number of people they saw living out of their cars on city streets in the past two years. The lot's first night of operation was last November, a couple of weeks after San Jose voters rejected a small property-tax increase that would have funded the construction of affordable housing.

It's just a patch of concrete adjacent to a community center where the kids can shower and do their homework, with a caseworker on site for a few hours every night, and a rent-a-cop security guard who occasionally cruises by to keep an eye on things. But Amador says her family feels safer here than on the street by themselves.

Every night at 7 p.m., she and her husband pull their two cars into the lot – the Explorer and an Econoline van sold to them by another homeless family. They pack their belongings under a tarp on the roof, lay the seats down, and go to sleep, waking up at the crack of dawn to repack the car so they can be off the lot by 7 a.m., when the community center's daytime crowd starts to show up. "I tell these [little] ones: 'We're living a learning experience,'" Amador says. "'I don't want you guys to go through this with your kids.'"

Housing has been one of San Jose Mayor Sam Liccardo's top priorities since he took office in 2015. When talking about it, he uses the local dialect, referring to solutions the city can "scale in a really disruptive way." The parking lot, though, is about as low-tech as it gets, which is how you can tell it wasn't originally part of the plan.

Four years ago, Liccardo set a goal to create housing for all of San Jose's 7,400 homeless. The city has just about hit that goal, sheltering 6,937 people this year. The problem, Liccardo explains, is "as quickly as we're housing residents, we're seeing three more getting pushed out into the street by the economy."

It isn't a failing economy that's putting residents out on the streets, though. It's a booming one. By almost every economic measure, the Bay Area is outperforming the rest of the nation. Together, the region's nine counties boast a GDP of $748 billion – larger than Switzerland's or Saudi Arabia's – and an economy that's growing at double the rate of the United States' at large. Santa Clara County, home to San Jose, has a job-growth rate that's twice the national one. But in the past five years, San Jose has built only one unit of housing for every six jobs it's created – a recipe for rising rents, rabid competition for available units, and, ultimately, economic evictions like the ones many of the families in the parking lot described when ROLLING STONE visited in March.

It's a dynamic happening across California, which, despite generating so much wealth, has the highest proportion of residents in poverty when you factor in the cost of living. San Diego, East Palo Alto, and L.A. have all opened safe parking lots in 2019; Mountain View and San Francisco are poised to follow suit, as demand for housing is far outstripping supply, and the resulting astronomical rents are pushing people out of homes and onto the streets.

"More and more people at higher and higher incomes are finding themselves with this cost burden, so as quickly as you fill up [new] units, you have more people falling into homelessness – oftentimes through economic evictions, where they can no longer afford the rent

increases," says Michael Lane, deputy director of the nonprofit Silicon Valley @ Home.

Almost all of the families sleeping in the parking lot in San Jose have stories that mirror Amador's: They grew up in the Bay Area, and despite holding down jobs – in warehouses, as customer-service reps, as call-center workers, in retail – they are struggling to find homes they can afford.

Twelve percent of the U.S. population lives in California, but it's home to nearly a quarter of the nation's homeless. In the spring, the results of a federal survey found rates of homelessness had increased by double digits across the state this year. In Los Angeles County, the rate went up 12 percent – 6,198 more people on the streets – and that was among the lowest percentage increases. Orange County saw a spike of 42 percent. In Alameda County, home to Oakland, homelessness was up 43 percent this year, and in the Central Valley's Kern County, it was up 50 percent.

California has been experiencing a "housing crisis" since at least the 1970s, but the situation has rapidly deteriorated in just the past few years. According to research by the *San Jose Mercury News*, in 2012, a family with an income of $100,000 could afford the median rent in 72 percent of Bay Area neighborhoods; as of 2018, the same family could afford the median rent in just 28 percent of those neighborhoods. Worse, there was not a single enclave in the Bay Area last year where a family with two parents working full-time making $15 an hour could afford the median rent.

CALIFORNIA LIVING
Christina Wade and Ray Adkins were lucky to find housing for their family after only two weeks in the San Jose parking lot. In 2018, there wasn't a single neighborhood in the Bay Area where two parents working full-time at $15 an hour could afford the median rent.

At its heart, California's housing problem is one of scarcity: According to one analysis, the state has 3.5 million fewer homes than it needs to house all the people who live there. That gap was created over decades – largely as a result of the zoning policies of individual communities, under pressure from local residents. Randy Shaw, a longtime Bay Area housing advocate and author of the book *Generation Priced Out,* says the best way to describe the dynamics at play is to look at the city of Atherton. Thirty minutes from San Jose, Atherton is the most expensive city in the country: The median price of a home there is $8.1 million.

"You can't build an apartment building in Atherton," Shaw says. City code prohibits anything other than a single-unit building with a footprint that cannot exceed 18 percent of the land. In other words, everything but a single, detached home with a yard is *verboten.* "You have all of these cities in California where you can't build anything but a luxury home," Shaw says. "When you have zoning restrictions that prevent you from building the housing you need, you're pretty much guaranteed to get in the situation we have."

It's a problem lawmakers across the state are grappling with, including in San Jose, where 94 percent of the city is zoned for single-family homes. "You got lots of family housing, and you're not going to bulldoze it to go build apartments," Liccardo said at a meeting of the state's mayors in July. "At least, not if you don't want [homeowners] to burn down City Hall."

IF THERE WERE ever a year in which California seemed poised to finally fix its housing crisis, it was this year. All of the conditions were in place: In November, voters elected Gov. Gavin Newsom, a Democrat who made ending the housing woes the central promise of his campaign, pledging to build 3.5 million homes by 2025. In the same election, Democrats solidified supermajorities in both chambers of the state Legislature – a virtual magic wand to pass any bills they wanted. In a signal of just how committed they were, the president pro tempore of the state Senate, Toni Atkins, created a new committee devoted exclusively to housing, and appointed San Francisco state Sen. Scott Wiener as its head.

Bearded and bespectacled, Wiener moved to the Bay Area in 1997, a 27-year-old gay man "coming to San Francisco for the same reason generations of LGBT people have come to San Francisco," he says. He flew out on a Friday night to look for an apartment. Early Saturday morning, he attended his first open house and was stunned to find there was already a line snaking around the block. "I said to myself, 'What on Earth is going on here?'"

Wiener eventually did find an apartment, and a job as a lawyer. On the side, he began doing pro bono work defending tenants – often older gay men and long-term HIV survivors who were facing no-fault evictions.

He was elected to his neighborhood association board and, later, to Harvey Milk's old seat on the San Francisco board of supervisors, roles that gave him a macro view of the dynamics that were contributing to San Francisco's housing quagmire. "The pieces all started coming together about why housing is so scarce, and why people are getting evicted, and why it takes years and years to approve new housing," Wiener says. He remembers sitting through the dozens of multihour meetings it took to approve the construction of a single zoning-compliant building – just one building – with affordable units. Meanwhile, San Francisco was emerging from a recession, and as more money flowed into the city, competition for the limited units available was intensifying and rents shot through the roof.

He won a seat in the California state Senate in 2016, arriving in Sacramento like a time traveler with grim tidings from the future. "I saw that other parts of California are headed to where San Francisco is," he says. "That San Francisco is five or 10 years ahead of other places – in a bad way. San Francisco went off the cliff first."

At the start of the legislative session this past January, the housing committee introduced a slate of bills focused on streamlining approvals for new construction, protecting renters, funding affordable housing, and, most controversially, reforming zoning laws. Wiener's top priority was SB50, an ambitious proposal that would prohibit cities from having zoning laws like Atherton's. Residential neighborhoods historically reserved for single-family homes would be opened up to multi-unit housing like triplexes and fourplexes. And even higher-density construction would be allowed around transit corridors and "job-rich" enclaves.

Wiener knew SB50 would be a battle, based on his earlier efforts at zoning reform, which were met with ferocious backlash from homeowners, NIMBY groups, and local politicians desperate to preserve "the character" of their communities. But nothing could have prepared him for the firestorm SB50 touched off.

At a meeting of the Beverly Hills City Council, the mayor compared "Sacramento politicians" like Wiener to King Haman, the biblical figure who ordered the slaughter of every Jew in his kingdom. The Coalition to Preserve L.A. called the bill "an act of war" declared by "our supreme rulers in the Cowtown Kremlin" – an act, they huffed, that would be "prohibited by the Endangered Species Act if California homeowners were considered a species worthy of protection." And an ugly mailer distributed in San Francisco even quoted the writer James Baldwin to suggest SB50 would negatively impact the city's black residents: "Urban renewal...means Negro removal," the mailer read. (It was roundly denounced by the head of the San Francisco NAACP, among others.)

But beyond the concerns attributed to wealthy suburban homeowners – that a proposed development would cast a shadow, blot out the sun, increase traffic, and, perhaps most to the point, impact the value of their homes, many of which have been dramatically appreciating in value as a direct result of the state's housing shortage – there are fears that the bill could inadvertently impact lower-income Californians already bearing the brunt of the housing crisis. Politicians in L.A. and San Francisco worry that permitting higher-density developments in urban centers would draw in high-priced projects, and drive out longtime residents. (SB50 requires new buildings with more

FAILED PROMISES Gov. Gavin Newsom campaigned on a promise to build 3.5 million units of housing by 2025. State Sen. Scott Wiener (right, behind Newsom) was put in charge of a new committee to address the housing crisis, but most of the proposed bills failed to pass.

than 11 units to include affordable housing, but developers can opt out by paying a fee instead.)

At the heart of the argument against SB50, from both ends of the economic spectrum, is a desire for "local control" and a belief that the people closest to the problem can diagnose it more accurately than lawmakers far removed from these communities. But arguments against a top-down measure like SB50 run up against the fact that cities, left to their own devices, have not built enough housing. And California's problem just keeps getting worse.

"You have more moderate suburban Democrats who, on many issues, are progressive," says Lane of Silicon Valley @ Home, "but when it comes to land use and zoning, [they want] local control – which means 'Just leave us alone, we understand there is a housing crisis, but we'll take care of it the way we want to take care of it' – which might mean doing very little."

By spring, despite a vocal campaign against it, SB50 was advancing through committee hearings quicker than anyone familiar with the plodding pace typical of housing legislation in Sacramento would expect. But in the middle of May, the bill's progress was abruptly halted – shelved without public discussion or a vote – by the head of the Senate appropriations committee: Sen. Anthony Portantino.

Portantino acknowledges he was the single person standing in the way of SB50, and makes no apologies for acting unilaterally. "I don't feel I would have been doing my duty without providing Californians this opportunity to take a

breath and get a better outcome," he tells ROLLING STONE. "I was in a position to help facilitate that better outcome. So I exercised my discretion to do that."

It's unusual for the head of one committee to single-handedly spike a piece of legislation, especially if it's the top priority of another committee head in your own party. To Lane and others, Portantino's decision signified something more than Democrat-on-Democrat violence. It was emblematic of a kind of generational warfare that pits the "younger and more diverse population in California," says Lane, "who have lots of student debt, are trying to rent an apartment, need to be in an urban environment near jobs, and are unable to find housing" against "an older generation of boomers who own their homes and resist multifamily housing, upzoning, and...are still a powerful force" in California politics.

Portantino is a homeowner in the small, wealthy bedroom community of La Cañada Flintridge, in the foothills of L.A., where the average home price is $1.7 million. But he bristles at the implication that those are the reasons he intervened to stop SB50. "My mom was a single mom, and I lived in a one-bedroom apartment with her – she gave me the bedroom and she slept on the couch," he says. "I get this stuff. But you've got to do it in a way that makes sense – and that's gonna pass."

The problem with SB50, he says, is not that it poses a threat to wealthy communities like his but that it would hurt "working-class cities, where families go for their first 1,100-square-foot affordable housing. Many of them are Latino communities, immigrant communities."

If SB50 passed, Portantino argues, developers would swoop in, erect market-rate buildings, and drive lower-income folks out, because "SB50 is not affordable housing...the lion's share of it is market-rate housing." Wiener has argued that "California as a whole needs every kind of housing," including for the middle class. Portantino rejects that logic: "Did trickle-down Reaganomics work? Did the recent tax cut for corporations trickle down to benefit the middle class and poor people? So why would you think this would work?"

Senate pro tem Toni Atkins insists that even without Portantino's shelving it, SB50 didn't have the votes. "I'm sure there are members who didn't want to vote on this bill," she says, "or were not ready to." But SB50 isn't dead yet – it will be under consideration again in January. Though if political pressure around it was high this year, it will be even higher in 2020, when a large share of state legislators will be up for re-election. Portantino and Wiener each see reasons to still be hopeful. "I think the reaction to the bill's delay made clear to everyone that there is a lot of public support, not just for SB50 but for pro-housing policies in general," says Wiener. After the bill was shelved, three different statewide polls showed [*Cont. on 96*]

The Eternal Sunshine *of* Harry Styles

Riding shotgun with the former boy-band hero as he opens up about sex, psychedelics, and becoming a 21st-century rock star

BY ROB SHEFFIELD

PHOTOGRAPHS BY RYAN McGINLEY

HARRY STYLES ISN'T EXACTLY dressed down for lunch. He's got a white floppy hat that Diana Ross might have won from Elton in a poker game at Cher's mansion circa 1974, plus Gucci shades, a cashmere sweater, and blue denim bell-bottoms. His nail polish is pink and mint green. He's also carrying his purse – no other word for it – a yellow patent-canvas bag with the logo CHATEAU MARMONT. The tough old ladies who work at this Beverly Hills deli know him well. Gloria and Raisa dote on him, calling him "my love" and bringing him his usual tuna salad and iced coffee.

He turns heads, to put it mildly, but nobody comes near because the waitresses hover around the booth protectively.

He was just a small-town English lad of 16 when he became his generation's pop idol with One Direction. When the group went on hiatus, he struck out on his own with his brash 2017 solo debut, whose lead single was the magnificently over-the-top six-minute piano ballad "Sign of the Times." Even people who missed out on One Direction were shocked to learn the truth: This pinup boy was a rock star at heart.

A quick highlight reel of Harry's 2019 so far: He hosted the Met Gala with Lady Gaga, Serena Williams, Alessandro Michele, and Anna Wintour serving an eyebrow-raising black lace red-carpet look. He is the official face of a designer genderless fragrance, Gucci's Mémoire d'une Odeur. When James Corden had an all-star dodgeball match on *The Late Late Show*, Harry got spiked by a hard serve from Michelle Obama, making him perhaps the first Englishman ever hit in the nads on TV by a first lady.

Closer to his heart, he brought down the house at this year's Rock & Roll Hall of Fame ceremony with his tribute to his friend and idol Stevie Nicks. "She's always there for you," Harry said in his speech. "She knows what you need: advice, a little wisdom, a blouse, a shawl." He added, "She's responsible for more running mascara – including my own – than all the bad dates in history." (Backstage, Nicks accidentally referred to Harry's former band as "'NSync." Hey, a goddess can get away with that sort of thing.)

Harry has been the world's It boy for nearly a decade now. The weirdest thing about him? He *loves* being this guy. In a style of fast-lane celebrity that takes a ruthless toll on the artist's personality, creativity, sanity, Harry is almost freakishly at ease. He has managed to grow up in public with all his boyish enthusiasm intact, not to mention his manners. He's dated a string of high-profile women – but he never gets caught uttering any of their names in public, much less shading any of them. Instead of going the usual superstar-pop route – en vogue producers, celebrity duets, glitzy club beats – he's gone his own way, and gotten more popular than ever. He's putting the finishing touches on his new album, full of the toughest, most soulful songs he's written yet. As he explains, "It's all about having sex and feeling sad."

The Harry Charm is a force of nature, and it can be almost frightening to witness in action. The most startling example might be a backstage photo from February taken with one of his heroes, Van Morrison. You have never seen a Van picture like this one. He's been posing for photos for 50 years, and he's been refusing to crack a smile in nearly all of them. Until he met Harry – for some reason, Van beams like a giddy schoolgirl. What did Harry do to him? "I was tickling him behind his back," Harry confides. "Somebody sent me that photo – I think his tour manager took it. When I saw it, I felt like John Travolta in *Pulp Fiction* opening the case with the gold light shining. I was like, 'Fuck, maybe I shouldn't show this to anyone.'"

In interviews, Harry has always tended to coast on that charm, simply because he can. In his teens, he was in public every minute and became adept at

guarding every scrap of his privacy. But these days, he's finding out he has things he wants to say. He's more confident about thinking out loud and seeing what happens. "Looser" is how he puts it. "More open. I'm discovering how much better it makes me feel to be open with friends. Feeling that vulnerability, rather than holding everything in."

Like a lot of people his age, he's asking questions about culture, gender, identity, new ideas about masculinity and sexuality. "I feel pretty lucky to have a group of friends who are guys who would talk about their emotions and be really open," he says. "My friend's dad said to me, 'You guys are so much better at it than we are. I never had friends I could really talk to. It's good that you guys have each other because you talk about real shit. We just didn't.'"

It's changed how he approaches his songs. "For me, it doesn't mean I'll sit down and be like, 'This is what I have for dinner, and this is where I eat every day, and this is what I do before I go to bed,'" he says. "But I will tell you that I can be really pathetic when I'm jealous. Feeling happier than I've ever been, sadder than I've ever been, feeling sorry for myself, being mad at myself, being petty and pitiful – it feels really different to share that."

At times, Harry sounds like an ordinary 25-year-old figuring his shit out, which, of course, he is. (Harry and I got to know each other last year, when he got in touch after reading one of my books, though I'd already been writing about his music for years.) It's strange to hear him talk about shedding his anxieties and doubts, since he's always come across as one of the planet's most confident people. "While I was in the band," he says, "I was constantly scared I might sing a wrong note. I felt so much weight in terms of not getting things wrong. I remember when I signed my record deal and I asked my manager, 'What happens if I get arrested? Does it mean the contract is null and void?' Now, I feel like the fans have given me an environment to be myself and grow up and create this safe space to learn and make mistakes."

> **Psychedelics have started to play a key role in Harry's creative process. "We were doing mushrooms, and I bit off part of my tongue," he says. "I was trying to sing with blood gushing out of my mouth."**

We slip out the back and spend a Saturday afternoon cruising L.A. in his 1972 silver Jaguar E-type. The radio doesn't work, so we just sing "Old Town Road." He marvels, "'Bull riding and boobies' – that is potentially the greatest lyric in any song ever." Harry used to be pop's mystery boy, so diplomatic and tight-lipped. But as he opens up over time, telling his story, he reaches the point where he's pitching possible headlines for this profile. His best: "Soup, Sex, and Sun Salutations."

How did he get to this new place? As it turns out, the journey involves some heartbreak. Some guidance from David Bowie. Some Transcendental Meditation. And more than a handful of magic mushrooms. But mostly, it comes down to a curious kid who can't decide whether to be the world's most ardently adored pop star, or a freaky artiste. So he decides to be both.

TWO THINGS ABOUT English rock stars never change: They love Southern California, and they love cars. A few days after Harry proclaimed the genius of "Old Town Road," we're in a different ride – a Tesla – cruising the Pacific Coast Highway while Harry sings along to the radio. "*Californiaaaaaa!*" he yells from behind the wheel as we whip past Zuma Beach. "It sucks!" There's a surprising number of couples along the beach who seem to be arguing. We speculate on which ones are breaking up and which are merely having the talk. "Ah, yes, the talk," Harry says dreamily. "Ye olde chat."

Harry is feeling the smooth Seventies yacht-rock grooves today, blasting Gerry Rafferty, Pablo Cruise, Hall and Oates. When I mention that Nina Simone once did a version of "Rich Girl," he needs to hear it right away. He counters by blowing my mind with Donny Hathaway's version of John Lennon's "Jealous Guy."

Harry raves about a quintessential SoCal trip he just tried: a "cold sauna," a process that involves getting locked in an ice chamber. His eyelashes froze. We stop for a smoothie ("It's basically ice cream") and his favorite pepper-intensive wheatgrass shot. It goes down like a dose of battery acid. "That'll add years to your life," he assures me.

We're on our way to Shangri-La studios in Malibu, founded by the Band back in the 1970s, now owned by Rick Rubin. It's where Harry made some of the upcoming album, and as we walk in, he grins at the memory. "Ah, yes," he says. "Did a lot of mushrooms in here."

Psychedelics have started to play a key role in his creative process. "We'd do mushrooms, lie down on the grass, and listen to Paul McCartney's *Ram* in the sunshine," he says. "We'd just turn the speakers into the yard." The chocolate edibles were kept in the studio fridge, right next to the blender. "You'd hear the blender going, and think, 'So we're all having frozen margaritas at 10 a.m. this morning.'" He points to a corner: "This is where I was standing when we were doing mushrooms and I bit off the tip of my tongue. So I was trying to sing with all this blood gushing out of my mouth. So many fond memories, this place."

It's not mere rock-star debauchery – it's emblematic of his new state of mind. You get the feeling this is why he enjoys studios so much. After so many years making One Direction albums while touring,

Contributing editor ROB SHEFFIELD *wrote about "Old Town Road" in the July issue.*

always on the run, he finally gets to take his time and embrace the insanity of it all. "We were here for six weeks in Malibu, without going into the city," he says. "People would bring their dogs and kids. We'd take a break to play cornhole tournaments. Family values!" But it's also the place where he has proudly bled for his art. *Mushrooms and Blood*. Now there's an album title."

Some of the engineers come over to catch up on gossip. Harry gestures out the window to the Pacific waves, where the occasional nude revelry might have happened, and where the occasional pair of pants got lost. "There was one night where we'd been partying a bit and ended up going down to the beach and I lost all my stuff, basically," he says. "I lost all my clothes. I lost my wallet. Maybe a month later, somebody found my wallet and mailed it back, anonymously. I guess it just popped out of the sand. But what's sad is, I lost my favorite mustard corduroy flares." A moment of silence is held for the corduroy flares.

Recording in the studio today is Brockhampton, the self-proclaimed "world's greatest boy band." Harry says hi to all the Brockhampton guys, which takes a while since there seem to be a few dozen of them. "We're together all the time," one tells Harry out in the yard. "We see each other all day, every day." He pauses. "You know how it is."

Harry breaks into a dry grin. "Yes, I know how it is."

One Direction made three of this century's biggest and best pop albums in a rush – *Midnight Memories, Four* and *Made in the A.M.* Yet they cut those records on tour, ducking into the nearest studio when they had a day off. 1D were a unique mix of five different musical personalities: Harry, Niall Horan, Louis Tomlinson, Zayn Malik, and Liam Payne. But the pace took its toll. Malik quit in the middle of a tour, immediately after a show in Hong Kong. The band announced its hiatus in August 2015.

It's traditional for boy-band singers, as they go solo and grow up, to renounce their pop past. Everybody remembers George Michael setting his leather jacket on fire, or Sting quitting the Police to make jazz records. This isn't really Harry Styles' mentality. "I know it's the thing that always happens. When somebody gets out of a band, they go, 'That wasn't me. I was held back.' But I don't feel like I was held back at all. It was so much fun. If I didn't enjoy it, I wouldn't have done it. It's not like I was tied to a radiator."

Whenever Harry mentions One Direction – never by name, always "the band" or "the band I was in" – he uses the past tense. It is my unpleasant duty to ask: Does he see 1D as over? "I don't know," he says. "I don't think I'd ever say I'd never do it again, because I don't feel that way. If there's a time when we all really *want* to do it, that's the only time for us to do it, because I don't think it should be about anything else other than the fact that we're all like, 'Hey, this was really fun. We should do this again.' But until that time, I feel like I'm really enjoying making music and experimenting. I enjoy making music this way too much to see myself doing a full switch, to go back and do that again. Because I also think if we went back to doing things the same way, it wouldn't be the same, anyway."

When the band stopped, did he take those friendships with him? "Yeah, I think so," he says. "Defi-

nitely. Because above all else, we're the people who went through that. We're always going to have that, even if we're not the closest. And the fact is, just because you're in a band with someone doesn't mean you have to be best friends. That's not always how it works. Just because Fleetwood Mac fight, that doesn't mean they're not amazing. I think even in the disagreements, there's always a mutual respect for each other – we did this really cool thing together, and we'll always have that. It's too important to me to ever be like, 'Oh, that's done.' But if it happens it will happen for the right reasons."

IF THE INTENSITY of the Harry fandom ever seems mysterious to you, there's a live clip you might want to investigate, from the summer of 2018. Just search the phrase "Tina, she's gay." In San Jose, on one of the final nights of his tour, Harry spots a fan with a homemade sign: "I'm Gonna Come Out to My Parents Because of You!" He asks the fan her name (she says it's Grace) and her mother's name (Tina). He asks the audience for silence because he has an important announcement to make: "Tina! She's *gaaaaay*!" Then he has the entire crowd say it together. Thousands of strangers start yelling "Tina, she's gay," and every one of them clearly means it – it's a heavy moment, definitely not a sound you forget after you hear it. Then Harry sings "What Makes You Beautiful." (Of course, the way things work now, the clip went viral within minutes. So did Grace's photo of Tina giving a loving thumbs-up to her now-out teenage daughter. Grace and Tina attended Harry's next show together.)

Harry likes to cultivate an aura of sexual ambiguity, as overt as the pink polish on his nails. He's dated women throughout his life as a public figure, yet he has consistently refused to put any kind of label on his sexuality. On his first solo tour, he frequently waved the pride, bi, and trans flags, along with the Black Lives Matter flag. In Philly, he waved a rainbow flag he borrowed from a fan up front: "Make America

Gay Again." One of the live fan favorites: "Medicine," a guitar jam that sounds a bit like the Grateful Dead circa *Europe '72*, but has a flamboyantly pansexual hook: "The boys and girls are in/I mess around with them/And I'm OK with it."

He's always had a flair for flourishes like this, since the 1D days. An iconic clip from November 2014: Harry and Liam are on a U.K. chat show. The host asks the oldest boy-band fan-bait question in the book: What do they look for in a date? "Female," Liam quips. "That's a good trait." Harry shrugs. "Not that important." Liam is taken aback. The host is in shock. On tour in the U.S. that year, he wore a Michael Sam football jersey, in support of the first openly gay player drafted by an NFL team. He's blown up previously unknown queer artists like King Princess and Muna.

What do those flags onstage mean to him? "I want to make people feel comfortable being whatever they want to be," he says. "Maybe at a show you can have a moment of knowing that you're not alone. I'm aware that as a white male, I don't go through the same things as a lot of the people that come to the shows. I can't claim that I know what it's like, because I don't. So I'm not trying to say, 'I understand what it's like.' I'm just trying to make people feel included and seen."

On tour, he had an END GUN VIOLENCE sticker on his guitar; he added a BLACK LIVES MATTER sticker, as well as the flag. "It's not about me trying to champion the cause, because I'm not the person to do that," he says. "It's just about not ignoring it, I guess. I was a little nervous to do that because the last thing I wanted was for it to feel like I was saying, 'Look at me! I'm the good guy!' I didn't want anyone who was really involved in the movement to think, 'What the fuck do you know?' But then when I did it, I realized people got it. Everyone in that room is on the same page and everyone knows what I stand for. I'm not saying I understand how it feels. I'm just trying to say, 'I see you.'"

'MAN CANNOT LIVE by coffee alone," Harry says. "But he will give it a damn good try." He sips his iced Americano – not his first today, or his last. He's back behind the wheel, on a mission to yet another studio – but this time for actual work. Today it's string overdubs. Harry is dressed in Gucci from head to toe, except for one item of clothing: a ratty Seventies rock T-shirt he proudly scavenged from a vintage shop. It says COMMANDER QUAALUDE.

On the drive over, he puts on the jazz pianist Bill Evans – "Peace Piece," from 1959, which is the wake-up tone on his phone. He just got into jazz during a long sojourn in Japan. He likes to find places to hide out and be anonymous: For his first album, he decamped to Jamaica. Over the past year, he spent months roaming Japan.

In February, he spent his 25th birthday sitting by himself in a Tokyo cafe, reading Haruki Murakami's *The Wind-Up Bird Chronicle*. "I love Murakami," he says. "He's one of my favorites. Reading didn't really used to be my thing. I had such a short attention span. But I was dating someone who gave me some books; I felt like I had to read them because she'd think I was a dummy if I didn't read them."

> "When someone gets out of a [boy] band, they go, 'That wasn't me,'" he says. "But it *was* me. And I don't feel like I was held back at all. If I didn't enjoy it, I wouldn't have done it. It's not like I was tied to a radiator."

A friend gave him Murakami's *Norwegian Wood*. "It was the first book, maybe ever, where all I wanted to do all day was read this," he says. "I had a very Murakami birthday because I ended up staying in Tokyo on my own. I had grilled fish and miso soup for breakfast, then I went to this cafe. I sat and drank tea and read for five hours."

In the studio, he's overseeing the string quartet. He has the engineers play T. Rex's "Cosmic Dancer" for them, to illustrate the vibe he's going for. You can see he enjoys being on this side of the glass, sitting at the Neve board, giving his instructions to the musicians. After a few run-throughs, he presses the intercom button to say, "Yeah, it's pretty T. Rex. Best damn strings I ever heard." He buzzes again to add, "And you're all wonderful people."

He's curated his own weird enclave of kindred spirits to collaborate with, like producers Jeff Bhasker and Tyler Johnson. His guitarist Mitch Rowland was working at an L.A. pizza shop when Harry met him. One of his closest collaborators is also one of his best friends: Tom Hull, a.k.a. Kid Harpoon, a longtime cohort of Florence and the Machine. Hull is an effusive Brit with a heart-on-sleeve personality. Harry calls him "my emotional rock." Hull calls him "Gary."

Hull was the one who talked him into taking a course on Transcendental Meditation at David Lynch's institute – beginning each day with 20 minutes of silence, which doesn't always come naturally to either of them. "He's got this wise-beyond-his-years timelessness about him," Hull says. "That's why he went on a whole emotional exploration with these songs." He's 12 years older, with a wife and kids in Scotland, and talks about Harry like an irreverent but doting big brother.

Last year, Harry was in the gossip columns dating the French model Camille Rowe; they split up last summer after a year together. "He went through this breakup that had a big impact on him," Hull says. "I turned up on Day One in the studio, and I had these really nice slippers on. His ex-girlfriend that he was really cut up about, she gave them to me as a present – she bought slippers for my whole family. We're still close friends with her. I thought, 'I like these slippers. Can I wear them – is that weird?'

"So I turn up at Shangri-La the first day and literally within the first half-hour, he looks at me and says, 'Where'd you get those slippers? They're nice.' I had to say, 'Oh, um, your ex-girlfriend got them for me.' He said, '*Whaaaat?* How could you wear those?' He had a whole emotional journey about her, this whole relationship. But I kept saying, 'The best way of dealing with it is to put it in these songs you're writing.'"

True to his code of gallant discretion, Harry doesn't say her name at any point. But he admits the songs are coming from personal heartbreak. "It's not like I've ever sat and done an interview and said, 'So I was in a relationship, and this is what happened,'" he says. "Because, for me, music is where I let that cross over. It's the only place, strangely, where it feels right to let that cross over."

The new songs are certainly charged with pain. "The stars didn't align for them to be a forever thing," Hull says. "But I told him that famous Iggy Pop quote where he says, 'I only ever date women who are going to fuck me up, because that's where the songs are.' I said, 'You're 24, 25 years old, you're in the eligible-bachelor category. Just date amazing women, or men, or whatever, who are going to fuck you up, and explore and have an adventure and let it affect you and write songs about it.'"

His band is full of indie rockers who've gotten swept up in Hurricane Harry. Before becoming his iconic drum goddess, Sarah Jones played in New Young Pony Club, a London band fondly remembered by a few dozen of us. Rowland and Jones barely knew anything about One Direction before they met Harry – the first time they heard "Story of My Life" was when he asked them to play it. Their conversation is full of references to Big Star or Guided by Voices or the Nils Lofgren guitar solo in Neil Young's "Speakin' Out." This is a band full of shameless rock geeks, untainted by industry professionalism.

In the studio, while making the album, Harry kept watching a vintage Bowie clip on his phone – a late-Nineties TV interview I'd never seen. As he plays it for me, he recites along – he's got the rap memorized. "Never play to the gallery," Bowie advises. "Never work for other people in what you do." For Harry, this was an inspiring pep talk – a reminder

not to play it safe. As Bowie says, "If you feel safe in the area that you're working in, you're not working in the right area. Always go a little further into the water than you feel you are capable of being in. Go a little bit out of your depth. And when you don't feel that your feet are quite touching the bottom, you're just about in the right place to do something exciting."

After quite a few hours, a bottle of Casamigos tequila is opened. Commander Quaalude pours the drinks, then decides what the song needs now is a gaggle of nonsingers bellowing the chorus. "Muppet vocals" is how he describes it. He drags everyone in sight to crowd around the mics. Between takes, he wanders over to the piano to play Harry Nilsson's "Gotta Get Up." One of the choir members, creative director Molly Hawkins, is the friend who gave him the Murakami novel. "I think every man should read *Norwegian Wood*," she says. "Harry's the only man I've given it to who actually read it."

It's been a hard day's night in the studio, but after-hours, everyone heads to a dive bar on the other side of town to see Rowland play a gig. He's sitting in with a local bar band, playing bass. Harry drives around looking for the place, taking in the sights of downtown L.A. ("Only a city as narcissistic as L.A. would have a street called Los Angeles Street," he says.) He strolls in and leans against the bar in the back of the room. It's an older crowd, and nobody here has any clue who he is. He's entirely comfortable lurking incognito in a dim gin joint. After the gig, as the band toasts with PBRs, an old guy in a ball cap strolls over and gives Rowland a proud bear hug. It's his boss from the pizza shop.

A FEW DAYS LATER, on the other side of the world: Harry's pad in London is lavish, yet very much a young single dude's lair. Over here: a wall-size framed Sex Pistols' album cover. Over there: a vinyl copy of Stevie Nicks' *The Other Side of the Mirror*, casually resting on the floor. He's having a cup of tea with his mum, Anne, the spitting image of her son, all grace and poise. "We're off to the pub," he tells her. "We're going to talk some shop." She smiles sweetly. "Talk some shit, probably," says Anne.

We head off to his local, sloshing through the rain. He's wearing a *Spice World* hoodie and savoring the soggy London-osity of the day. "Ah, Londres!" he says grandly. "I missed this place." He wants to sit at a table outside, even though it's pouring, and we chat away the afternoon over a pot of mint tea and a massive plate of fish and chips. When I ask for toast, the waitress brings out a loaf of bread roughly the size of a wheelbarrow. "Welcome to England," Harry says.

He's always had a fervent female fandom, and, admirably, he's never felt a need to pretend he doesn't love it that way. "They're the most honest – especially if you're talking about teenage girls, but older as well," he says. "They have that bull-shit detector. You *want* honest people as your audience. We're so past that dumb outdated narrative of 'Oh, these people are girls, so they don't know what they're talking about.' They're the ones who *know* what they're talking about. They're the people who listen obsessively. They fucking own this shit. They're running it."

He doesn't have the uptightness some people have about sexual politics, or about identifying as a fem-

Harry's Favorite Things

What does a young superstar spend his time thinking about? Classic rock, mostly, but also Quentin Tarantino

Van Morrison

"It's my favorite album ever," Harry says of *Astral Weeks*. "Completely perfect." On his first tour, before going onstage, he'd play "Madame George" — Morrison's tender 10-minute ballad for a Belfast drag queen.

Wings

Paul McCartney's 1970s band left a slew of shaggy art-pop oddities. Harry swears by *London Town* and *Back to the Egg*. "In Tokyo I used to go to a vinyl bar, but the bartender didn't have Wings records. So I brought him *Back to the Egg*. 'Arrow Through Me' was the song I had to hear every day when I was in Japan."

'Pulp Fiction'

The 1994 Tarantino movie blew his mind growing up. "I watched it when I was too young," he admits. "But when I was 13, I saved up money from my paper route to buy a 'Bad Mother Fucker' wallet. Just a stupid white kid in the English countryside with that wallet."

Joni Mitchell

Harry got so obsessed with her 1971 classic, *Blue*, he went on a quest. "I kept hearing her dulcimer all over *Blue*. So I tracked down the lady who built Joni's dulcimers." He even got his own personal dulcimer lesson.

Crosby, Stills and Nash

These three hippie balladeers summed up the mellow West Coast soft-rock vibe. "Those harmonies, man," Harry says. "'Helplessly Hoping' is the song I would play if I had three minutes to live. It's one of my one-more-time-before-I-go type of songs."

inist. "I think ultimately feminism is thinking that men and women should be equal, right? People think that if you say 'I'm a feminist,' it means you think men should burn in hell and women should trample on their necks. No, you think women should be equal. That doesn't feel like a crazy thing to me. I grew up with my mum and my sister – when you grow up around women, your female influence is just bigger. Of course men and women should be equal. I don't want a lot of credit for being a feminist. It's pretty simple. I think the ideals of feminism are pretty straightforward."

His audience has a reputation for ferocity, and the reputation is deserved. At last summer's show at Madison Square Garden, the floor was wobbling during "Kiwi" – I've been seeing shows there since the 1980s, but I'd never seen that happen before. (The only other time? His second night.) His bandmates admit they feared for their lives, but Harry relished it. "To me, the greatest thing about the tour was that the room became the show," he says. "It's not just me." He sips his tea. "I'm just a boy, standing in front of a room, asking them to bear with him."

That evening, Fleetwood Mac take the stage in London – a sold-out homecoming gig at Wembley Stadium, the last U.K. show of their tour. Needless to say, their most devoted fan is in the house. Harry has brought a date: his mother, her first Fleetwood Mac show. He's also with his big sister Gemma, bandmates Rowland and Jones, a couple of friends.

He's in hyperactive-host mode, buzzing around his cozy VIP box, making sure everyone's champagne glass is topped off at all times. As soon as the show begins, Harry's up on his feet, singing along ("Tell me, tell me *liiiiies!*") and cracking jokes. You can tell he feels free – as if his radar is telling him there aren't snoopers or paparazzi watching. (He's correct. This is a rare public appearance where nobody spots him and no photos leak online.) It's family night. His friend Mick Fleetwood wilds out on the drum solo. "Imagine being that cool," Gemma says.

Midway through the show, Harry's demeanor suddenly changes. He gets uncharacteristically solemn and quiet, sitting down by himself and focusing intently on the stage. It's the first time all night he's taken a seat. He's in a different zone than he was in a few minutes ago. But he's seen many Fleetwood Mac shows, and he knows where they are in the set. It's time for "Landslide." He sits with his chin in hand, his eyes zeroing in on Stevie Nicks. As usual, she introduces her most famous song with the story of how she wrote it when she was just a lass of 27.

But Nicks has something else she wants to share. She tells the stadium crowd, "I'd like to dedicate this to my little muse, Harry Styles, who brought his mother tonight. Her name is Anne. And I think you did a really good job raising Harry, Anne. Because he's really a gentleman, sweet and talented, and, boy, that appeals to me. So all of you, this is for you."

As Nicks starts to sing "Landslide" – "I've been afraid of changing, because I built my life around *youuuu*" – Anne walks over to where Harry sits. She crouches down behind him, reaches her arms around him tightly. Neither of them says a word. They listen together and hold each other close to the very end of the song. Everybody in Wembley is singing along with Stevie, but these two are in a world of their own. ®

The Strange Birth and Near Death of Weezer

25 years after the Blue Album, Weezer's past and present members look back at their origin story

BY BRIAN HIATT

IN THE SPRING OF 1990, Rivers Cuomo was 19 years old, and all of his plans were coming undone. The year before, he and his high school metal band, Avant Garde, moved from suburban Connecticut to L.A., all five members crammed into the same filthy studio apartment, sleeping on the floor. Cuomo was the lead guitarist, with an arsenal of squeal-y virtuoso licks and hair so long and majestically poufed-up that it essentially served as the band's sixth member. Flamboyance aside, Cuomo left frontman duties to an operatically inclined friend. "I could have seen myself in the NBA as easily as being a lead singer in a metal band," Cuomo says now. "That's just, like, unthinkable."

Avant Garde gave themselves a slightly less embarrassing new name, Zoom, and streamlined their music, though they still sounded like a more proggy, less-fun Dokken. Cuomo tried easing up on the hair spray. None of

it helped them find favor in a metal scene so overcrowded with dreamers that Sunset Strip sidewalks were lined with discarded band fliers at night. Even worse, it was all about to fade away, in tandem with the decade that spawned it.

Thirty years later, Cuomo sits in his Santa Monica home studio, which is filled with sunlight and plants, and overlooks a Zen garden outside. His wife and two kids are upstairs; his mom lives in a house he bought for her next door. He's wearing a plaid shirt with the sleeves rolled up, gray jeans, and no glasses, which makes him almost hard to recognize. We're listening to his heavy chugging on Zoom's "Street Life," with piercing vocals from his school friend Kevin Ridel. Cuomo grins, picks up an acoustic guitar (a compact Ed Sheeran signature model, for some reason), and riffs along, chuckling when the song shifts into an oddball funk feel in the verses.

IN MY ROOM

Rivers Cuomo (left) and Brian Bell, L.A., 1994

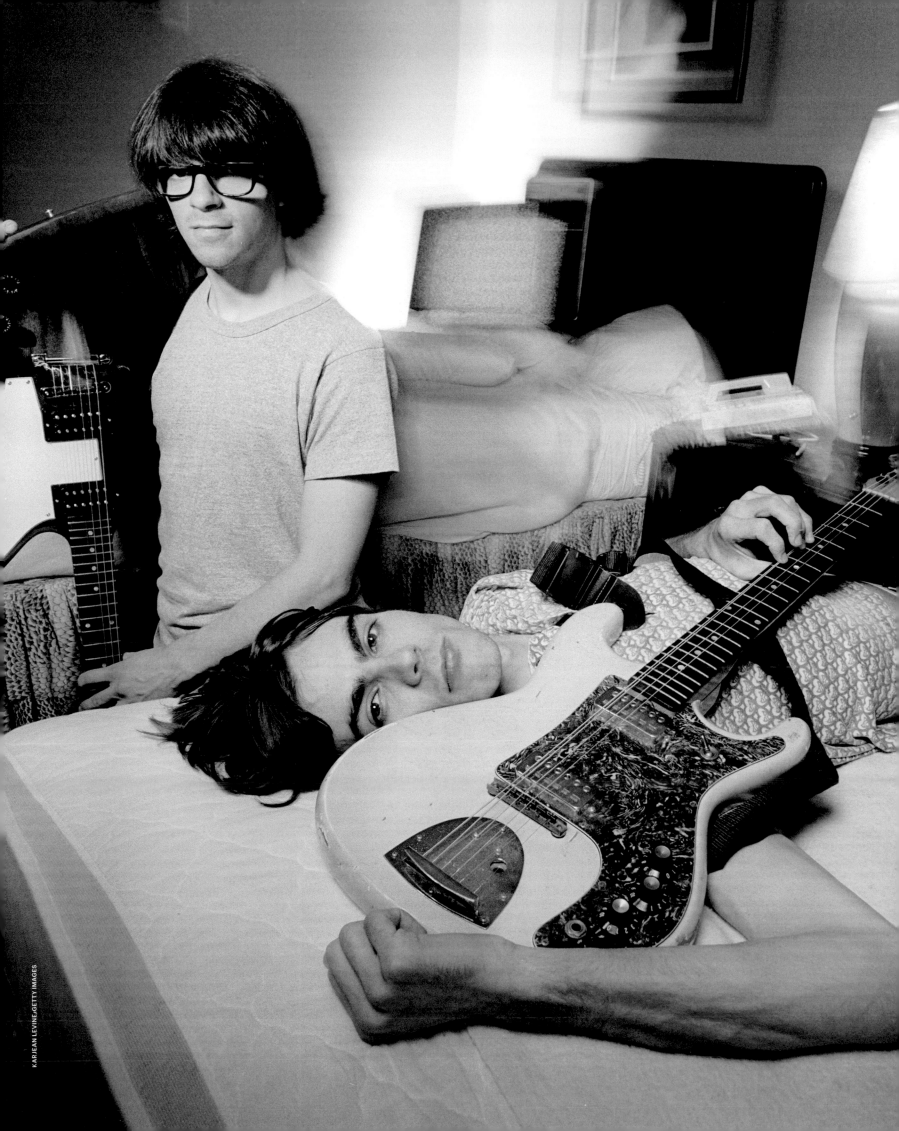

Around the time Zoom began to fizzle out, Cuomo got some bad news from the Guitar Institute of Technology, the trade school for shredders he was supposed to be attending. Cuomo was educated in an ashram before the culture shock of public school at age 11, and had always been a gifted and disciplined student. But he was overwhelmed by the excitement of playing gigs and skateboarding around Hollywood, which he saw as "the center of the universe."

"I couldn't bring myself to get into diligent-student mode," he says. When G.I.T. administrators told him he was "basically expelled," he was crushed, begging them to take him back, mostly because he felt terrible about wasting his parents' money. He still seems to regret it, though he's amused at the notion that he may well be the only person on Earth to flunk out of the Guitar Institute of Technology and later graduate from Harvard.

Faced with all these failures, "my system of values was crumbling," as he later wrote in a college application. "I was thinking of myself as a lead guitar player, thinking that faster harmonic minor scales equals better," he says. "Thinking that I could move out to L.A. with Avant Garde and we were just going to be huge rock stars. Then seeing one band member after another leave, abandon me, and not being able to hold it together or put it back together." There were nasty breakups, too, "heartbreak with two girlfriends, back to back."

When Weezer eventually emerged with a major-label debut in 1994, a shorn and oft-bespectacled Cuomo at their helm, it seemed like they had emerged "out of nowhere," as a then-suspicious Stephen Malkmus of Pavement puts it; he recalls raising his eyebrows at the "Pixies/Pavement-y sound" of a band with zero indie releases to its name. (He says he's now a fan.) The guys from the Chicago alt-band Urge Overkill wondered aloud to one band member, in all seriousness, if Weezer's record label put them together, Monkees-style. Weezer's young fans, unconcerned with indie cred (or unaware it existed), were entirely unbothered, but many critics shared the skepticism, in an era when subtle distinctions between different brands of guitar rock seemed all-consuming and identity-defining.

"People see us now as this credible band, and they assume we always were credible," says Cuomo. "But, man, we could not have been more hated on when we came out." He's never forgotten a local newspaper referring to the band as "Stone Temple Pixies," the idea being "Stone Temple Pilots were a corporate copy of all of the cool grunge bands, and we were a corporate copy of the Pixies."

In a way, Weezer did come out of nowhere. They exist only because of the small miracle of Rivers Cuomo's impossibly fast reinvention, abetted by meeting just the right collaborators at just the right time. If Weezer's detractors had seen a picture of Cuomo circa 1989, they would have considered their worst suspicions confirmed. Weezer would far outlast their initial critics, surviving long enough to win a whole new wave of them. They inspired countless emo bands, made two classic albums in a row, and became one of their era's most indefatigable acts, tunneling through styles and decades with output of

Senior writer BRIAN HIATT *wrote the "Game of Thrones" cover story in April.*

varying quality in a manner more akin to the Isley Brothers or Jefferson Airplane/Starship than any of their own alt-peers. (Their lineup has been admirably stable, too – current bassist Scott Shriner is still the new guy after 18 years.)

Weezer's self-titled debut, a.k.a. the Blue Album, is one of the most enduring artifacts of the alt-rock age, winning teenage hearts in generation after generation, not unlike Green Day's *Dookie,* released a few months earlier. It's the geeky, equally angsty little brother of *Ten* and *Nevermind,* somehow both more sincere and more ironic than its predecessors, and in some ways bolder in its disregard for the old rules of rock; Kurt Cobain liked Marvel Comics too, but he never sang about Kitty Pryde and Nightcrawler, as Cuomo does in "In the Garage."

By 1991, not much more than a year after Zoom's demise, Cuomo was writing what would become the first Weezer songs; he still had his metal hair when the band played its first shows. In the space of 16 months or so, Cuomo would utterly transform his musical value system, learn to write hit songs, start singing lead vocals, and find a whole new set of bandmates. And by 1995, he would already be sick of it all. "As I get older," says drummer Pat Wilson, "everything seems weirder, and more strange and unlikely. And that's kind of how I look at Weezer."

T ALL STARTED AT Tower Records, where Cuomo got a job while taking classes at Los Angeles City College. At Tower, he met a punk-rock dude named Pat Finn who would hook him up with his future bandmates, and introduce him to a new world of music. Cuomo knew metal, and had a quiet soft spot for pop – Madonna, Tiffany. Practically everything else was alien to him. "At first I just could not get into it at all," he says. "It sounded like garbage to me. Velvet Underground; *Pet Sounds* was reissued around that time. 13th Floor Elevators, Pixies, Sonic Youth, it all sounded like noise. I thought, 'None of this is catchy.' But I

> "There was a worry that 'Buddy Holly' would become the 'Detachable Penis' of the album," says former Weezer bassist Matt Sharp. "We sensed it could be seen as a novelty song, and people wouldn't take the album seriously."

came to love it all. Now I don't understand how I missed it."

He would become a serious Beatles and Beach Boys fan; on his bookshelf is a copy of Brian Wilson's 1991 autobiography overflowing with Cuomo's notations. But a much newer band was his greatest influence. Nirvana's *Bleach,* and the 1990 single "Sliver," with its sugary melody combined with uncharacteristic-for-rock lyrics ("Grandma, take me home"), were transformative.

Cuomo first heard "Sliver" at Tower, shelving CDs as he took it in. "It's like, 'Oh, my God. This is so beautiful to me. And I identify with it so much.' Hearing him sing about Mom and Dad and Grandpa Joe, these personal family issues, in a really heartbreaking kind of innocent, childlike way. Over these straightforward chords in a major key. But then the distortion kicks in, and he starts screaming. Shit! That's what I want to do." Cuomo took continual influence from Nirvana; the "In Bloom" video, where Kurt Cobain wears thick glasses, helped Cuomo feel comfortable in his own, according to founding guitarist Jason Cropper.

Pat Finn connected Cuomo with Pat Wilson, an endearingly goofy, cherubic They Might Be Giants and Van Halen fan with serious drum skills, albeit in a stripped-down style that initially baffled Cuomo. Their first jam session went nowhere. They took another stab at it after Cuomo moved in with Wilson and his friend Matt Sharp, an arty, brainy dude with gothy, Anglophile tastes, and a weird dyed rat tail left over from his own longhaired days. He had his own musical projects, and was, at that point, just a roommate, with a remarkably lucrative day job telemarketing upscale dog shampoo.

Cuomo and Wilson started a band called Fuzz, enlisting a young woman named Scottie Chapman on bass. Cuomo's first songwriting efforts included "The Answer Man," which sounds like a grungier Jane's Addiction – Cuomo is obviously trying to sing like Perry Farrell, pushing his range, adding some grit to his voice, even cursing in the lyrics. It's solid, though; you could imagine this band getting signed. "It was maybe eight months into the band that I started singing much more simply," Cuomo says, "as I had sung in choir in high school. It was the strangest thing. I was like, 'Wait, you can just sing, like, with your normal voice? Over a rock band, and it will work?'"

After one or two Fuzz shows, Chapman quit, apparently going on to star on the show *Mythbusters.* She now works as a dental hygienist. "She realized we were idiots," says Wilson, laughing. "Rivers and I had a lot of facility on our instruments. She was like, 'These guys are nerds.' We were *totally* nerds. Rivers was smart enough to realize, 'I need to not look like a nerd.' I never gave a shit. I just wanted to play."

Wilson was such a geek in his own right, or Cuomo's camouflage was so effective, that the drummer initially mistook Cuomo for a "Valley metal jock, like Dan Cortese on MTV's *Rock N' Jock*" – he loved playing basketball and rode his bike everywhere. There's at least one picture of Cuomo wearing bicycle shorts onstage looking quite Axl-ish. In truth, Cuomo was much like he is now: blazingly intense but quiet and internal, prone to unsettlingly long conversational pauses; he conveys the impression that social interaction is work for him, but also that he can enjoy

HAIR TODAY
Above: The newly formed Weezer, 1992 (clockwise from left: Jason Cropper, Pat Wilson, Matt Sharp, and Rivers Cuomo).

FADE TO BLUE
Right: Weezer around the Blue Album's release. Brian Bell (second from right) replaced Cropper just as they finished the LP.

OUT OF THE GARAGE
Left: Weezer recording the Blue Album in 1993. Recalls drummer Wilson, "We were totally nerds. Rivers was smart enough to realize, 'I need to not look like a nerd.' I never gave a shit. I just wanted to play."

IN DREAMS
Right: An early album-cover sketch, complete with band logo

the effort, workaholic that he is. (When I visit him in June, he's spent the morning writing computer code for fun.)

After Fuzz came Sixty Wrong Sausages, with Cuomo, Wilson, and Finn on bass, along with a second guitarist, a guy named Jason Cropper. Cropper was, unlike everyone else, a California native, and a chill, cheerful guy – qualities that would ultimately spell trouble amid the odder personalities. "He was this more unbridled, Northern California punk hippie spirit," Cuomo says now. "Which is so different from my careful, controlled artistry." Cuomo wasn't the focus of Sixty Wrong Sausages; it was more of a collective, and it didn't last long.

Cuomo decided he would write 50 songs in a row before allowing himself to form another band or play live again. He moved to Santa Monica, started attending college there, and recorded demo after demo on an eight-track cassette recorder. He wrote only 30 or so songs, but among them were "Undone – The Sweater Song" and other eventual Weezer tracks. Cropper says that around this time, Cuomo also made an entire, never-released rap album under the name Vegeterrorists – songs about his lifelong vegetarianism in styles akin to Public Enemy and Run-DMC. "Rivers can drop mad beats and spit mad rhymes with the best," says Cropper. "And if I stayed in the band, we would've done records like that years ago." (The only released evidence of this period is a striking demo of Cuomo covering Ice Cube's "The Bomb" like a one-man Rage Against the Machine.)

Matt Sharp had moved to the Bay Area, and was embarking on weekslong, aimless Amtrak rides. On one of those trips, he listened to a tape of Cuomo's new songs that Wilson had slipped him. When he heard "Sweater Song" and the breakup lament "The World Has Turned and Left Me Here," everything changed. "Rivers was able to articulate something that up to that point had been elusive for me," says Sharp, who immediately decided to put all of his energy in service of Cuomo's songs, making plans to move back to L.A. "I thought, 'I'm doing this, no matter what has to be done to make it happen,'" Sharp says. "'We're on this journey together.'"

Cuomo was profoundly affected by Sharp's enthusiasm. "I think Matt called me and said, 'You're a genius. I'm going to be your bass player. We're going to be a band.' It confirmed all my greatest hopes for myself. Knowing he felt so strongly about the songs was all the confidence I needed."

Cuomo also got a boost from Jennifer Chiba, his "quasi-girlfriend" at the time. After getting dumped twice, Cuomo was protective of his feelings – and, less sympathetically, "had every hope I was going to be this huge rock star, and have all these other options for girlfriend/wife. Still, she was the coolest thing. She was three years older, the first half-Japanese girl I met. She turned me on to Flaming Lips and Sebadoh, and did wonders for my confidence, saying, 'All the hipsters are going to think you're the coolest.' She's like, 'You're going to be cuter if you cut your hair.' That was the first time any girl had said that. Until then it was always, 'No, don't cut your hair.'"

Sharp essentially became the band's manager. "Rivers had put his trust in me to act as the band's *consigliere*," says Sharp. "As Tom Hagen to Cuomo's Corleone, it was my obligation to try to create an environment that allowed him to tune out extraneous noise so he could keep the focus squarely on his writing." Though he would go on to become a hit songwriter, Sharp wasn't really a co-writer in Weezer, but still helped shape their aesthetic, in part just by spending hours talking with Cuomo. Initially, the as-yet-unnamed Weezer had some leftover Fuzz songs in their set list – Cuomo saw them as key to the group's sound – but Sharp's lack of enthusiasm for them helped push them out. "And I think that's where Matt's head was at, at the time," recalls Wilson. "'Yeah, let's not be grunge. Let's be more like the Beach Boys. But loud.'"

Cuomo, who had reverted back to his studiousness post-G.I.T., got an offer for a generous scholarship at UC-Berkeley, with a stipend, an apartment, even a parking space. He gave Sharp a year to get them a record deal; otherwise he would take Berkeley's offer. Weezer played their first show on March 19th, 1992, a month after forming, on Valentine's Day. Cuomo persuaded a club, Raji's, to let them play – they ended up on a bill with Keanu Reeves' then-band, Dogstar, as a late-night closer. [*Cont. on 97*]

When you hear that a famous musician has kids, you have to wonder: What was it like growing up in *that* house? We talked to the progeny of rap legends like Ol' Dirty Bastard and the Notorious B.I.G. about summer vacations with Usher, seeing your dad on the cover of tabloids, and getting your deceased father's cane back from the LAPD

Children of Rap

Riding the Coaster With O.D.B.

The Three Kids of Ol' Dirty Bastard

Taniqua Jones
DOB 4/23/88
HOMETOWN Bed-Stuy, Brooklyn
CALLING Craft specialist for the disabled; cast member, *Growing Up Hip Hop New York*; co-director of the estate of Russell Jones (otherwise known as O.D.B.)

Barsun Jones
a.k.a. Young Dirty Bastard
DOB 4/9/89 **HOMETOWN** Bed-Stuy
CALLING Entrepreneur

Shaquita Jones
DOB 3/11/92
HOMETOWN Bed-Stuy **CALLING** Mother; DeVry MBA student; co-director of the estate of Russell Jones

THE MOMENT THEY KNEW THEIR DAD WAS FAMOUS "He came to my classroom because I was bad in school," Barsun says. "He was supposed to set me right, but as soon as he came, teachers started acting different and classmates started participating in his celebrity. So now being bad for me was good: He was in the room."

O.D.B.'S FAVORITE ROLLER COASTER "He would take us to Six Flags all the time," says Taniqua, "and Coney Island. He loved the Cyclone. He was always just our daddy. He was famous, but he never changed for no-body. He never faked the funk."

THE DOWNSIDE OF BEING YOUNG DIRTY BASTARD "For me," Barsun says, "having O.D.B. as a pops was real hard. People thought I was rich, and I was not — when he got locked up, we wasn't really making too much money. I was never rich until I made myself rich."

KEEPING THE LOVE ALIVE "After my father passed," says Taniqua, "I was 16, and Method Man brought me onstage. He said, 'This is Taniqua, O.D.B.'s firstborn seed.' Every-body in the crowd went crazy, and I just started crying to see how much love people had for my father. You couldn't even see how many people held up their W's out of respect for him."

THE O.D.B. LEGACY "People see this crazy person on TV," says Taniqua, who manages the O.D.B. estate with Shaquita. "People don't know he's my father and tell me he was a crack addict. We want people to know what he brought to Wu-Tang. We organized a concert last year for his birthday — oh, my God, you never realize how much it takes. But next, we're trying to set up a tour."

THIS SPREAD: HAIR AND MAKEUP BY MELONY LEWIS; STYLING BY JAMILA GREEN; CLOTHING BY CHECKS & BALANCES

PHOTOGRAPHS BY BRAD OGBONNA | BY KIANA FITZGERALD

Taniqua (left),
Barsun,
and Shaquita

Wu-Tang Family Values

Prana Supreme Diggs
Daughter of RZA

DOB 8/1/00 **HOMETOWN** Los Angeles **CALLING** Creative director for 36 Chambers Clothing; singer in duo Americana, with her mother, Tekitha

THE MOMENT SHE KNEW HER DAD WAS FAMOUS "This kid I went to school with [in eighth grade] had told people that my dad was *his* dad. It was at that moment that I realized other people my age knew my dad, and that he was so cool that other people wanted him to be their dad. I was like, 'OK, he's different.'"

PERKS OF HAVING THE LEADER OF THE WU-TANG CLAN IN THE HOUSE "When I was 10, my siblings and I were going through this phase where we had a little band. It didn't go past the house, of course — well, it went as far as the guesthouse, which had a studio in it. Dad produced some beats for us, and my older brother hopped on the guitar while me and my sister sang. Dad made it feel like we were some real artists in the studio, recording a hit single."

THE RZA LEGACY "I work at 36 Chambers, the clothing and record company, but on the clothing side. I also do Americana music as a mother-daughter duo. My dad's craft comes in the dedication that he has — he's always improving his artistic muscle. His love and appreciation and dedication — that he knows he can grow no matter what — is what I take to other parts of my life."

Growing Up in Run's House

Daniel Simmons
Son of Rev Run

DOB 3/21/95 **HOMETOWN** Queens **CALLING** Rapper; actor **THE MOMENT HE KNEW HIS DAD WAS FAMOUS** "As a kid, I would go to concerts and be like, 'Everybody's dad can't be doing this....'" **BONDING WITH THE REVEREND** "When I was in middle school, he'd take me to the skate park every weekend — something he might not have ever had an interest in." **OTHER PERSONAL MEMORIES OF HIS POPS** "I'm not sure [I have any], because I grew up on a show with my dad [reality series *Run's House*]." **POST-*RUN'S HOUSE* GIG** "I act on the television show *Grown-ish*, make music, and march to the beat of what I enjoy." **WHY PEOPLE STOP HIM IN THE STREET** "They come up and tell me about my dad's significance to hip-hop, and what he did with Adidas: being the first rap act to have an endorsement deal."

From BK to the Runway

T'yanna Wallace
Daughter of the Notorious B.I.G.

DOB 8/10/93 **HOMETOWN** Stroudsburg, Pennsylvania **CALLING** Designer and owner, Notoriouss Clothing
THE MOMENT SHE KNEW HER DAD WAS FAMOUS "I was probably five or six — that's when you kind of get the vibe and say, 'OK, I see him on TV.' So you get the idea he's not a regular dad. But you realize how famous your dad is when *you're* getting recognized and you've never even been in the industry."
BIGGIE'S NONMUSICAL HOBBIES "My dad didn't just rap, he could draw. I didn't get the musical skills, but I can draw — that's how I got into sketching and fashion."
HAS SHE SEEN THE DRAWINGS? "No."
THE FINE LINE BETWEEN HONORING YOUR FATHER AND FORGING YOUR OWN WAY "I have a clothing line, Notoriouss Clothing, which I started my sophomore year of college. I wanted to pursue something that was inspired by my dad so I could continue the legacy. But even though the name is influenced by my dad, Notoriouss is not a Biggie line — he has his own merch line. This is not that."
WHAT C.J. THINKS ABOUT HIS HALF SISTER'S CLOTHING LINE "I've always admired her for attacking that."
B.I.G. RESPONSIBILITY "I really want my kids to understand my dad's legacy and what I did to continue it. And I want them to be able to do the same thing. I want my kids to know how big their grandfather is."

The Notorious D.A.D.

C.J. Wallace
Son of the Notorious B.I.G. (and Faith Evans)

DOB 10/29/96 **HOMETOWN** Los Angeles **CALLING** Founder, cannabis brand Think BIG **EARLIEST MEMORY OF BIGGIE** "There were pictures of [the Notorious B.I.G., who died before C.J.'s first birthday], but it never clicked that was my dad. His face looked threatening." **THE HEIRLOOM HE WANTS BACK** "My grandmother told me that the cane my dad had when he passed away is still in LAPD possession after 20 years. I want to retrieve it." **THE B.I.G. LEGACY** "My dad said that the options for most black men were wicked jump shots or slinging crack rocks. Even today, it's not often that people see a young black man that started his own company. I want to be a voice for my generation who says we don't all have to be rappers or play sports, or fall into the wrong lane with the wrong people."

DOB 6/15/94
HOMETOWN Jamaica, Queens
CALLING CEO, Lipmatic cosmetics; actress

GROWING UP NAS "My house was the center — every party, every dinner. It felt like it was always all about my parents and me."

THE MOMENT SHE KNEW HER DAD WAS FAMOUS "I reached for candy in the checkout line at the supermarket, and my dad was on a magazine. When I started saying, 'That's Dad!' my mom hushed me."

BEST SUMMER VACATION "Dad was promoting *Stillmatic* with Usher. I would sit on a little box at the side of the stage and give him a thumbs-up. And he would give me a thumbs-up back, like, 'OK, I'm good.'"

THE WEIRD MIDDLE GROUND "If your parent is a rap star, they didn't come from money. You're the first generation who experiences money, going to private school. It's this weird middle ground: You're not really from that private-school world, but you're not from where your parent is from. You get the street smarts, but you also get opportunities. It's the best of both worlds."

An Illmatic Childhood

Destiny Jones
Daughter of Nas

SINCE 1828

COURVOISIER.

YOU'VE ARRIVED
WHEN YOU ALL ARRIVE.

HONOR · YOUR · CODE

Can We Survive Extreme Heat?

Humans have never lived on a planet this hot, and we're totally unprepared for what's to come

BY JEFF GOODELL

PHOTO ILLUSTRATION BY SEAN McCABE

On a scorching day in downtown Phoenix,

when the temperature soars to 115°F or higher, heat becomes a lethal force. Sunshine assaults you, forcing you to seek cover. The air feels solid, a hazy, ozone-soaked curtain of heat. You feel it radiating up from the parking lot through your shoes. Metal bus stops become convection ovens. Flights may be delayed at Sky Harbor International Airport because the planes can't get enough lift in the thin, hot air. At City Hall, where the entrance to the building is emblazoned with a giant metallic emblem of the sun, workers eat lunch in the lobby rather than trek through the heat to nearby restaurants. On the outskirts of the city, power lines sag and buzz, overloaded with electrons as the demand for air conditioning soars and the entire grid is pushed to the limit. In an Arizona heat wave, electricity is not a convenience, it is a tool for survival.

As the mercury rises, people die. The homeless cook to death on hot sidewalks. Older folks, their bodies unable to cope with the metabolic stress of extreme heat, suffer heart attacks and strokes. Hikers collapse from dehydration. As the climate warms, heat waves are growing longer, hotter, and more frequent. Since the 1960s, the average number of annual heat waves in 50 major American cities has tripled. They are also becoming more deadly. Last year, there were 181 heat-related deaths in Arizona's Maricopa County, nearly three times the number from four years earlier. According to the Centers for

Contributing editor JEFF GOODELL *wrote about the Paris Agreement in January.*

Disease Control and Prevention, between 2004 and 2017, about a quarter of all weather-related deaths were caused by excessive heat, far more than other natural disasters such as hurricanes and tornadoes.

Still, the multiplying risks of extreme heat are just beginning to be understood, even in places like Phoenix, one of the hottest big cities in America. To Mikhail Chester, the director of the Metis Center for Infrastructure and Sustainable Engineering at Arizona State University, the risk of a heat-driven catastrophe increases every year. "What will the Hurricane Katrina of extreme heat look like?" he wonders aloud as we sit in a cafe near the ASU campus. Katrina, which hit New Orleans in 2005, resulting in nearly 2,000 deaths and more than $100 billion in economic damage, demonstrated just how unprepared a city can be for extreme climate events.

"Hurricane Katrina caused a cascading failure of urban infrastructure in New Orleans that no one really predicted," Chester explains. "Levees broke. People were stranded. Rescue operations failed. Extreme heat could lead to a similar cascading failure in Phoenix, exposing vulnerabilities and weaknesses in the region's infrastructure that are difficult to foresee."

In Chester's view, a Phoenix heat catastrophe begins with a blackout. It could be triggered any number of ways. During periods of extreme heat, power demand surges, straining the system. Inevitably, something will fail. A wildfire will knock out a power line. A substation will

blow. A hacker might crash the grid. In 2011, a utility worker doing routine maintenance near Yuma knocked out a 500-kilovolt power line that shut off power to millions of people for up to 12 hours, including virtually the entire city of San Diego, causing economic losses of $100 million. A major blackout in Phoenix could easily cost much more, says Chester.

But it's not just about money. When the city goes dark, the order and convenience of modern life begin to fray. Without air conditioning, temperatures in homes and office buildings soar. (Ironically, new, energy-efficient buildings are tightly sealed, making them dangerous heat traps.) Traffic signals go out. Highways gridlock with people fleeing the city. Without power, gas pumps don't work, leaving vehicles stranded with empty tanks. Water pipes crack from the heat, and water pumps fail, leaving people scrounging for fresh water. Hospitals overflow with people suffering from heat exhaustion and heatstroke. If there are wildfires, the air will become hazy and difficult to breathe. If a blackout during extreme heat continues for long, rioting, looting, and arson could begin.

And people will start dying. How many? "Katrina-like numbers," Chester predicts. Which is to say, thousands. Chester describes all this coolly, as if a Phoenix heat apocalypse is a matter of fact, not hypothesis.

"How likely is this to happen?" I ask.

"It's more a question of when," Chester says, "not if."

EXTREME HEAT IS the most direct, tangible, and deadly consequence of our hellbent consumption of fossil fuels. Rising carbon-dioxide levels in the atmosphere trap heat, which is fundamentally changing our climate system. "Think of the Earth's temperature as a bell curve," says Penn State climate scientist Michael Mann. "Climate change is shifting the bell curve toward the hotter end of the temperature scale, making extreme-heat events more likely." As the temperature rises, ice sheets are melting, seas are rising, hurricanes are getting more intense, rainfall patterns are changing (witness the recent flooding in the Midwest). Drought and flooding inflict tremendous economic damage and create political chaos, but extreme heat is much more likely to kill you directly. The World Health Organization predicts heat stress linked to the climate crisis will cause 38,000 extra deaths a year worldwide between 2030 and 2050. A recent study published in *Nature Climate Change* found that by 2100, if emissions continue to grow, 74 percent of the world's population will be exposed to heat waves hot enough to kill. "The more warming you have, the more heat waves you have," says Michael Wehner, a scientist at Lawrence Berkeley National Laboratory. "The more heat waves you have, the more people die. It's a pretty simple equation."

Heat waves are driven not just by rising temperatures but by a change in the dynamics of

TOO HOT TO HANDLE
Volunteers distribute water on a sweltering day in Phoenix, where the average temperature is rising faster than in almost every other American city. There were 181 heat-related deaths in Arizona's Maricopa County last year.

the Earth's climate system. As the atmosphere warms, the temperature difference between the poles and the subtropics is shrinking, which is changing the path of the jet stream, the big river of wind 35,000 feet up in the sky that drives our weather system. The jet stream's path is shaped by atmospheric waves called Rossby waves, which are created naturally as the Earth spins. Mann explains that as the Earth's temperature gradient flattens, the Rossby waves tend to bend, resulting in a curvy jet stream that is more likely to get "stuck," trapping weather systems in place and creating what Mann calls "huge heat domes."

Extreme heat is already transforming our world in subtle and not-so-subtle ways. Disney executives recently voiced concern that rising temperatures will significantly reduce the number of visits to their parks. In Germany, officials were forced to put a speed limit on the autobahn because of fears the road would buckle from heat. The U.S. military has already incurred as

much as $1 billion in costs during the past decade – from lost work, retraining, and medical care – due to the health impacts of heat. The warming of the planet "will affect the Department of Defense's ability to defend the nation and poses immediate risks to U.S. national security," a recent DOD report said. Forests and soils are drying out, contributing to explosive and unprecedented wildfires. Habitation zones for plants and animals are changing, forcing them to adapt to a warmer world or die. A U.N. report found that 1 million species are at risk of extinction in the coming decades. Another study by researchers at MIT suggests that rising temperatures and humidity may make much of South Asia, including parts of India and Pakistan, too hot for human existence by the end of the century. As scientist Peter Gleick, co-founder of the Pacific Institute in California, told me, "There is a shocking, unreported, fundamental change coming to the habitability of many parts of the planet, including the USA."

Since the Industrial Revolution, the Earth's temperature has risen by 1.8°F (1°C). As we burn more fossil fuels, the warming is accelerating. The planet's average surface temperature in 2018 was the fourth-highest since 1880, when record-keeping began. Gavin Schmidt, a climate scientist at NASA, said there's a "90 percent chance" that 2019 will turn out to be even hotter. Nine of the 10 warmest years in recorded history have occurred since 2005. This past June was the hottest June ever recorded. Astonishingly, July was the hottest month in human history.

But warming is not happening at the same rate everywhere. The Arctic, for example, is warming twice as fast as the rest of the world. Why? It's a classic climate feedback loop: Ice and snow are highly reflective, bouncing sunlight back into space. But as the region warms, sea and land ice declines, exposing more open land and ocean, which are darker and absorb more heat. As temperatures rise, the permafrost melts, which releases methane, a potent greenhouse gas, which further accelerates the melting. Greenland is in the midst of one of the biggest melt seasons ever recorded, with temperatures as much as 40°F above normal. And as the Arctic heats up and dries out, it burns. There have been unprecedented wildfires this year, with more than 100 massive fires raging across the region since June. The burning peat has already emitted more than 100 million tons of greenhouse gases (nearly the annual carbon emissions of Belgium), further accelerating the climate feedback cycle that's cooking the planet.

But the greatest risk to human health may be in areas that are already hot, where temperature increases will strain habitability. In the U.S., the fastest-warming cities are in the Southwest. Las Vegas, El Paso, Tucson, and Phoenix have warmed the most, each by at least 4.3°F since 1970. Globally, many of the hottest cities are in India. In May, a deadly heat wave sent temperatures above 120°F in the north. The desert city of Churu recorded a high of 123°F, nearly breaking India's record of 123.8°F, set in 2016. There were warnings not to go outside after 11 a.m. Authorities poured water on roads to keep them from melting. A 33-year-old man was reportedly beaten to death in a fight over water. The preliminary death toll in India for this summer's heat wave is already more than 200, and that number is likely to grow.

How hot will it get? That depends largely on how far and how fast carbon-dioxide levels rise, which depends on how much fossil fuel the world continues to burn. The Paris Climate Agreement (which President Trump pulled the U.S. out of) aims to limit the warming to 3.6°F (2°C). Given the current trajectory of carbon pollution, hitting that target is all but impossible. Unless nations of the world take dramatic action soon, we are headed for a warming of at least 5.4°F (3°C) by the end of the century, making the Earth roughly as warm as it was 3 million years ago during the Pliocene era, long before Homo sapiens came along. "Human beings have literally never lived on a planet as hot as it is today," says Wehner. A 5.4°F-warmer world would be radically different from the one we know now, with cities swamped by rising seas and epic droughts turning rainforests into deserts. The increased heat alone would kill significant numbers of people. A recent report from the University of Bristol estimated that with 5.4°F of warming, about 5,800 people could die each year in New York due to the heat, 2,500 could die in Los Angeles, and 2,300 in Miami. "The relationship between heat and mortality is clear," Eunice Lo, a climate scientist at the University of Bristol and the lead author of the report, tells me. "The warmer the world becomes, the more people die."

THE PROPERTIES OF HEAT confused scientists and philosophers for centuries. In Greek mythology, heat was controlled by Ankhiale, the goddess of warmth. Eighteenth-century chemist Antoine Lavoisier believed heat was an invisible fluid, known as the caloric, that flowed from hotter bodies to colder bodies. It wasn't until the mid-19th century that scientists understood that when you feel heat, what you're really feeling is energy released by the vibration of molecules. The faster something vibrates, the higher its temperature, and the more energy it releases. The sun is a big ball of hydrogen that burns at about 10,000°F and releases vast amounts of energy into space, which travels in the form of waves until colliding with something, such as a rock or a building or a human being. That, in turn, speeds up the vibrations within that object. These accelerating vibrations are what we humans sense as "getting hotter."

Not surprisingly, heat regulation is one of the body's most important functions. One way to think about the human body is as a giant multicellular heat engine that strives to maintain a constant internal state of 98.6°F. The very process of living – of eating, breathing, moving, thinking, having sex – generates heat. The outside air is usually lower than 98.6°F, so our bodies release heat, mostly by circulating blood to capillaries close to the surface of our skin, where

the heat can be dissipated (that's why your body is warm to the touch). Without a cooling mechanism, just our basic metabolism would result in about a 2°F hourly rise in body temperature. We wouldn't even make it through the day.

If the equilibrium between body temperature and the outside world gets too far out of whack, the body quickly deploys its only emergency heat-release system: It sweats. For sweating to be effective, however, the water has to evaporate. High humidity is uncomfortable (and potentially deadly) because the air, already filled with water, has little capacity to add more, so the sweat simply sits on the surface.

The loss of water through sweat is itself a health hazard. The average person contains roughly 40 liters of fluid. On a hot day, when the body is struggling to keep from overheating, a person can easily lose a liter of sweat per hour. When the body is down one liter, basic functions are impaired. When it's down five, fatigue and dizziness set in. Ten liters disturbs hearing and vision and you will likely collapse – a condition known as heat stress.

But if it's hot and humid enough, even drinking plenty of water won't help. As the body's temperature rises, it tries to cool itself by pumping more and more blood to capillaries under the skin. The heart pumps faster, the chest pounds, the pulse races. As the body loses water, our blood becomes thicker and harder to propel. When the body temperature hits 103°F or so, the metabolism will be running flat out in an emergency effort to dump heat. Eventually, the most vital organs can't keep up, and the body's neurological system begins to collapse. At 105°F, the body is in serious trouble. The brain swells, often causing hallucinations and convulsions. Pupils become dilated and fixed. Sweating stops, and the skin feels hot and dry to the touch. At that point, if the body temperature isn't lowered immediately by emergen-

cy cooling measures such as being packed in ice or a plunge into cold water, the person could die of heatstroke.

The psychological impacts of extreme heat are obvious to anyone who's ever felt cranky on a hot day. But the impacts go beyond crankiness. When temperatures rise, suicide rates can go up at a pace similar to the impact of economic recessions. Some aspects of higher cognition are impaired. School test scores decline, with one study showing decreases across five measures of cognitive function, including reaction times and working memory.

The link between heat and violence is particularly intriguing. "There is growing evidence of a psychological mechanism that is impacted by heat, although we can't yet say exactly what that is," says Solomon Hsiang, a professor of public policy at Berkeley. Some scientists speculate that higher temperatures impact neurotransmitters in the brain, resulting in lower levels of serotonin, which has been shown to lead to aggressive behavior. So rising heat may literally alter the chemistry in our brains. One study showed that police officers were more likely to fire on intruders during training exercises when it was hot. Andrew Shaver, a professor of political science at the University of California, Merced, analyzed data about conflicts in Afghanistan and Iraq and found that attacks by insurgents involving RPGs and assault rifles increased with higher temperatures, while planned attacks did not. "During conflicts, higher temperatures seem to provoke more impulsive aggression," Shaver says. One speculative paper projects that by 2099, due to rising heat, the U.S. could see an additional 22,000 murders, 180,000 rapes, 3.5 million assaults, and 3.76 million robberies, burglaries, and acts of larceny.

THE CITY OF PHOENIX has no master plan to deal with heat, no radical remaking of the building codes or zoning laws in place, and no heat czar who is in charge of reimagining the city for the 21st century. Re-engineering a city like Phoenix for extreme heat is a long-term project that has only just begun, says David Hondula, a senior sustainability scientist at Arizona State University. "Think about places like Minnesota, and what they have done to engineer for cold winters," Hondula says. "They have tunnels you walk through in the winter, the heating systems are optimized, you drive cars with snow tires and all-wheel drive. We have done nothing like that in Phoenix, or in any city, really, when it comes to thinking about heat. The whole idea of engineering for extreme heat is still in its infancy."

Retrofitting Phoenix – including reining in suburban sprawl, revising building codes to improve energy efficiency and ventilation, and creating greener urban spaces – is certainly imaginable, but "if we are going to be serious about this, a big investment is required," Hondula says. "We need billions of dollars."

38,000

Extra deaths predicted to occur per year because of extreme heat between 2030 and 2050, according to the World Health Organization

28%

How much less productive the U.S. economy is on days above 86°F, according to a recent study

5,684

Number of people who died from heat in the U.S. between 2004 and 2017

"We have elected officials who don't believe in climate change," says a Phoenix activist. "How do you get effective policy if people are pushing against it because they're batshit crazy?"

HOTTER AND HOTTER

July 2019 was the hottest month on the planet, in more than 100 years of record-keeping. Below is a snapshot of one of the hottest days in the U.S., when virtually the entire country was sweltering. "This is not your grandfather's summer," said U.N. Secretary-General António Guterres.

HEAT WAVE | JULY 19TH, 2019

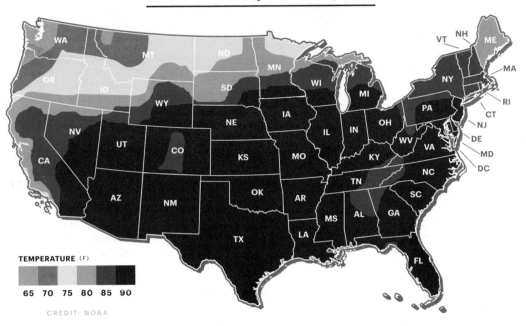

TEMPERATURE (F)

65 70 75 80 85 90

CREDIT: NOAA

EARTH'S INCREASING AVERAGE SURFACE TEMPERATURE

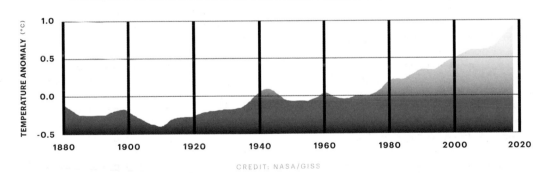

CREDIT: NASA/GISS

It will also require leadership from city and state officials. A recent poll found that two-thirds of Arizonans accept that climate change is happening, but most elected officials in the state, including Republican Gov. Doug Ducey, are hardly climate activists. Arizona is one of the sunniest states in the nation, and yet only 6.5 percent of the state's electricity comes from solar power. A statewide ballot initiative in 2018 to require 50 percent renewable power by 2030 was soundly defeated, in part because the parent company of Arizona Public Service, the big public utility in the state, spent more than $37 million on false and misleading arguments about how transitioning to renewable power would raise power bills and destroy the Arizona economy.

"We have a large number of elected officials who don't believe in climate change, period," says Stacey Champion, a longtime Phoenix energy and climate activist. "How do you get effective, data-driven policy if you have people pushing hard against it because they are batshit crazy, or they are afraid it will spook companies like Nike who want to come here?"

But as the world heats up, cities will get the worst of it. They are built of concrete and asphalt and steel, materials that absorb and amplify heat during the day, then radiate it out at night. Air conditioners blow out hot air, exacerbating the problem of urban heat buildup. Downtown Phoenix, for example, can be as much as 21°F hotter than the surrounding area.

This phenomenon, which is called Urban Heat Island Effect, impacts most cities in the world. On average, cities are 2 to 5°F warmer than their leafy suburbs during the day – and as much as 22°F warmer during some evenings. The effect is so pervasive that some climate skeptics have seriously claimed that global warming is merely an illusion created by thousands of once-rural meteorological stations becoming surrounded by urban development.

Counterintuitively, the biggest health effects of rising heat often occur at night, when vulnerable people such as the elderly badly need the chance to cool down. Without that chance, they can succumb to heatstroke, dehydration, and heart attacks. This appears to be what happened during the heat wave that hit Europe in 2003, killing 70,000 people, mostly in buildings without air conditioning. Research has shown that the cause of many deaths was not so much the 104°F daytime temperatures, but the fact that nights stayed in the seventies or higher.

To reduce the heat-absorbing impacts of urban areas, some cities are experimenting with white roofs. The idea is to change the reflectivity of the rooftop to bounce more light off so that the building absorbs less heat. New York, for instance, introduced rules on white roofs into its building codes as long ago as 2012. Volunteers and workers have taken white paint to 10 million square feet of roofs in the city, though that is still less than one percent of New York's total roof area.

Keith Oleson of the National Center for Atmospheric Research in Boulder, Colorado, looked at what might happen if every roof in large cities around the world were painted white. He found it could decrease the Urban Heat Island Effect by a third – enough to reduce the maximum daytime temperatures by about 1°F, and even more in hot, sunny regions such as the Arabian Peninsula and Brazil.

In Los Angeles, city officials are experimenting with asphalt sealants that give roads a light-reflective surface. Manufacturers claim they can reduce the surface temperature by up to 30°F. Greg Spotts, chief sustainability officer in the Los Angeles Bureau of Street Services, says the sealants have worked well so far, but cost (it's roughly three times more expensive than conventional sealant) and questions about durability have limited their use. Spotts estimates that of the 23,000 miles of streets in L.A., less than 10 miles have been covered with reflective coating. "But we know it works, because dogs always move over to walk on the white streets when they can," says Spotts.

Other places, such as Stuttgart, Germany, are trying to re-engineer the airflow of the whole city. Stuttgart is an industrial town surrounded by steep hills at the bottom of a river valley, where heat and polluted air linger. To help cool things off, city planners have built a number of wide, tree-flanked arterial roads that work as ventilation corridors and help clean, cool air flow down from the hills. Officials have also restricted new buildings from going up on certain hillsides in order to keep the air moving.

Many urban centers are trying to combat heat the old-fashioned way: by planting shade trees. Since 2011, Louisville, Kentucky, has planted about 100,000 trees. Paris Mayor Anne Hidalgo has plans to create "urban forests" in the center of the city. In May, I visited Singapore, a tropical city that is far more densely developed than Phoenix. It's hard to find a single inch of Singapore that is in any way "natural," but since the 1960s, there has been a deliberate government-led effort to green the city. The highways are canopied with lush trees, urban parks have been expanded, and thousands of sidewalk trees have been planted. Wandering downtown, I felt like I was in a jungle, there were so many vines and plants hanging from windows.

"There used to be a lot of nice big shade trees in Phoenix, but they cut them all down in the 1960s because they were worried about how much water they used," Mark Hartman, Phoenix's chief sustainability officer, says with a bit of an eye roll. (In fact, climate-appropriate trees like mesquite or ash only require extra water for the first year or two after they're planted – when they get bigger, the increased shade often increases soil moisture by reducing evaporation.) In 2010, as the problems of extreme heat became more obvious, Phoenix officials set a goal of doubling the percentage of the city covered with tree canopy from 12 to 25 percent. Then came the inevitable budget cuts and layoffs after the recession. According to Hartman, "Tree planting was cut back to stay only slightly ahead of those lost to storms and drought." Today, the tree-canopy cover in Phoenix remains virtually unchanged from what it was a decade ago.

But if you look closely, you can find signs that a few people in Phoenix are starting to think differently about life in a rapidly warming world. You will hear about plans for "walkable shade corridors." Most commercial buildings are now constructed with white roofs. At one light-rail stop, you can push a button and get sprayed with a cool mist of water while you wait for the train. One Phoenix city official has been known to walk around downtown passing out umbrellas on hot days. And the city launched an aggressive social media campaign to alert people to the risks of extreme heat.

But mostly what you see in Phoenix is asphalt and concrete, cars and malls, and big, crowded highways. In this sense, it is like virtually every other city in America, except with a few more palm trees (which are purely decorative – they provide zero shade) and a heavy dependence on air conditioning. As Hondula says one afternoon as we drive through Encanto Village, a historic middle-class neighborhood in Phoenix, "The number-one heat adaptation here is forking over money for the electric bill."

IN RESEARCH LABS around the country, you can find experiments with walls engineered to suck heat out of buildings, and wood that's altered to be stronger, cooler, and better for insulation. But right now, the only technology deployed at scale against extreme heat is air conditioning. Nearly 90 percent of the homes in America have it – it's as necessary as running water and a toilet.

Without air conditioning, the world as we know it today wouldn't exist. It's inconceivable that there would be a city of 4.5 million people living in the middle of the Southwestern desert – much less 20 million people living in Florida – without air conditioning. After World War II, Americans flocked from chilly Northern states to sunny Southern states. It was one of the great demographic shifts of the 20th century, and it precisely mirrored the proliferation of air conditioners. "Air conditioning was essential to the development of the Sun Belt," historian Gary Mormino has argued. "It was unquestionably the most significant factor."

Air conditioning is one of those paradoxical modern technologies that creates just as many problems as it solves. For one thing, it requires

12.5

Billions of tons of ice melted in Greenland on August 1st, 2019, the single largest loss since scientists began tracking in 1950

10%

Percentage of global energy consumption used for air conditioning and fans

250

Average number of large wildfires (1,000 acres or bigger) a year in the Western United States, a 78 percent increase from 1989

a lot of energy, most of which comes from fossil fuels. AC and fans already account for 10 percent of the world's energy consumption. Globally, the number of air-conditioning units is expected to quadruple by 2050. Even accounting for modest growth in renewable power, the carbon emissions from all this new AC would result in a more than 0.9°F increase in global temperature by the year 2100.

Cheap air conditioning is like crack cocaine for modern civilization, keeping us addicted and putting off serious thinking about more creative (and less fossil-fuel-intensive) solutions. Air conditioning also creates a kind of extreme heat apartheid. If you're rich, you have a big house with enough air conditioning to chill a martini. And if you are poor, like Leonor Juarez, a 46-year-old single mother whom I met on a recent July afternoon when the temperature was hovering around 115°F, you live in South Phoenix, where sidewalks are dirt and trees are few, and you hope you can squeeze enough money out of your paycheck to run the AC for a few hours on hot summer nights.

On hot days, Juarez's small apartment feels like a cave. She has heavy purple curtains on the windows to block the sun. "I could not live here without air conditioning," she tells me. Because she has poor credit, she doesn't qualify for the usual monthly billing from Salt River Project, her utility. Instead, to pay for electricity and keep her AC running, SRP has given her a card reader that plugs into an outlet that she has to feed like a jukebox to keep the power on. Juarez turns on her AC only a few hours a day – still, her electric bill can run $500 a month during the summer, which is more than she pays for rent. To Juarez, who takes a bus five miles to a laundromat in the middle of the night because washing machines are discounted to 50 cents a load after 1 a.m., $500 is a tremendous amount of money.

She shows me the meter on the card reader: She has $49 worth of credit on it, enough for a few more days of power. And when that runs out? "I am in trouble," she says bluntly. Juarez, who works as an in-home caretaker for the elderly, says she knows of several people who lived alone and died when they failed to pay their electric bills and tried to live without AC.

One such woman was named Stephanie Pullman, a 72-year-old retiree who lived alone on a fixed income of less than $1,000 a month in a small house in Sun City West, a development north of downtown Phoenix. Last summer, she was late to pay her electric bill and owed $176.84. On September 5th, 2018, Pullman paid $125, leaving $51.84 unpaid. Two days later, when the temperature hit 107°F, her electric company, Arizona Public Service, cut off her power. A week later, Pullman's daughter became worried when she hadn't heard from her mother, who had a heart condition, so she alerted locals. A Maricopa County Sheriff's officer entered the house and found Pullman dead in her bed. Cause of death: heat exposure.

The real question is not whether superheated cities are sustainable. With enough money and engineering, you could sustain life on Mars. The issue is, sustainable for whom?

RECORD-BREAKING HEAT

Year after year in the 21st century, we're seeing unprecedented temperatures — with nine of the 10 hottest years on record happening since 2000. And as the Earth warms from ever-rising carbon-dioxide levels, the temperatures grow increasingly extreme, with deadly consequences.

Churu, India
HIGHEST TEMP 123°F

Churu, a city of more than 100,000 in the desert west of New Delhi, was the epicenter of a brutal heat wave that swept through northern India in early June. City officials had to pour water on roads to prevent them from melting. People were advised not to go outside after 11 a.m., and doctors canceled vacations to care for heat-stressed residents. Early estimates put the national death toll above 200 people, but that number is likely to grow.

Anchorage, Alaska
HIGHEST TEMP 90°F

On July 4th, temperatures in Anchorage hit an all-time high, breaking the previous record by 5°F. The city canceled Independence Day fireworks out of fear they could spark wildfires, which have been raging through the Arctic on an unprecedented scale this season. Sea-ice cover in the nearby Bering Sea was the lowest on record, and recent marine heat waves have contributed to unusually high mortality rates in whales and other Arctic species.

Gallargues-le-Montueux, France
HIGHEST TEMP 114.6°F

June 28th was the hottest day in French history, with the town of Gallargues-le-Montueux in southern France clocking the highest temperature. Paris broke its own record in July, reaching 108.6°F. In 2003, a heat wave killed 15,000 people in France. To avoid repeating that disaster, officials installed temporary water fountains and portable pools in Parisian neighborhoods and distributed 5,000 water bottles to the homeless.

San Francisco
HIGHEST TEMP 100°F

San Francisco is known for cool, breezy summer days. Not this year. In early June, a heat wave roasted the West Coast, pushing the temp to 100°F in San Francisco during the hottest June on record. Commuter train tracks warped in the heat, and blackouts left thousands of Bay Area residents without power. Temperature records were broken throughout the state, with Salinas reaching 105°F, and the town of Thermal, near San Diego, reaching 113°F.

Alert, Nunavut, Canada
HIGHEST TEMP 70°F

Alert is the northernmost settlement in the world, about 500 miles from the North Pole, a land of ice and polar bears and military bases. In mid-July, the temperature hit a beachy 70°F, the highest ever recorded there; it usually averages about 44°F in July. "It's really quite spectacular — this is unprecedented," said David Phillips, chief climatologist for Environment Canada, who added, "Our models for the rest of the summer are saying, 'Get used to it.'"

In 2018, APS cut off power to customers more than 110,000 times. Of those, more than 39,000 were during the blistering months of May through September.

Pullman's death sparked wide media coverage and street protests over APS's disconnect policy, and pushed Arizona regulators to ban power shut-offs on hot summer days. (APS shut-offs have been linked to at least two other heat-related deaths in recent years.) These deaths also raise larger questions about the future of cities like Phoenix. As temperatures soar in the coming years, the real question is not whether superheated cities are sustainable. With enough money and engineering skill, you can sustain life on Mars. The issue is, sustainable for whom?

HEAT IS NOT AN EQUAL-opportunity killer. If you're poor, sick, old, or homeless, you're more likely to die during a heat wave. Recent immigrants, both legal and undocumented, are particularly at risk. A 2017 study published in the *American Journal of Public Health* found that immigrants are three times more likely than citizens to die from heat-related illnesses. More than 85 percent of non-U.S. citizens who died from heat-related causes were Hispanic. Researchers hypothesized that working outdoors and in agriculture increased vulnerability.

In Arizona, the most visible victims of heat are the homeless. One afternoon, I drive around Glendale, a town just outside Phoenix, with Brian Farretta and Rich Heitz of the Phoenix Rescue Mission, a faith-based group dedicated to getting people off the streets. Recently, the group launched "Code: Red," an initiative to pass out water and other essentials to people on the street during heat waves. "Our strategy is simple," Heitz says. "We find people and give them water."

Heitz, 48, has lived in Arizona most of his adult life. He is a gentle man with a goatee and a Harley-Davidson cap. Before joining the Phoenix Rescue Mission, Heitz spent 10 years on the streets of Phoenix as a heroin addict. "I lost myself in numbness," he says. He spent a few years in jail for various charges and has now gone clean and is devoting his life to helping others do the same.

We pull into Sands Park, a typical suburban green swath with basketball courts and picnic areas. Heitz and Farretta head to a concrete bathroom, where they find a middle-aged woman sitting in the shade on the floor near the entrance.

She has brown, sunburned skin, long gray hair, and a pleasant smile. She's dressed in dirty jeans and a T-shirt. Beside her is what looks like a children's coloring book. On the cover, written in red crayon, are the words "It's Raining Love."

"How are you doing, Sherri?" Heitz asks her. "You doing OK in the heat?"

I notice her face is flushed, and there are rings of sweat under her arms.

"Yeah, I'm keeping cool." [Cont. on 96]

Reviews

A NEW KIND OF OUTLAW COUNTRY

Four excellent female artists get together for a groundbreaking supergroup album

By WILL HERMES

The Highwomen

The Highwomen

ELEKTRA

★★★★☆

THE HIGHWOMEN come steeped in history – a history they rewrite, literally and figuratively. Their name, and the title track of their terrific self-titled debut, alludes to "The Highwayman," Jimmy Webb's 1977 song-turned-hit signature of the Highwaymen, the Eighties supergroup of Johnny Cash, Willie Nelson, Waylon Jennings, and Kris Kristofferson. Rewritten with Webb for a new singer-songwriting collective – Brandi Carlile, Maren Morris, Amanda Shires, and Natalie Hemby – "The Highwomen" swaps the original's mythic male narratives for female ones: an immigrant mom who dies fleeing Honduras through Mexico, a "witch" hanged in Salem, ➡

ILLUSTRATION BY
Bijou Karman

→ THE HIGHWOMEN

a murdered Freedom Rider, a preacher persecuted for her gender. "We are the highwomen, we sing of stories still untold/We carry the sons you can only hold," the women declaim over sparkling guitars. It's as powerful as musical storytelling gets.

What's most impressive about *The Highwomen,* handsomely produced with Nashville neoclassicist Dave Cobb, is how artfully, and matter-of-factly, it engages social issues. Credit the concentration of songwriting talent. Every woman here is at the top of her game. With last year's *By the Way, I Forgive You,* Carlile reached a new creative peak after 13 years of record-making. Morris is a boundary-breaking pop-country hit machine. Shires is a fiddle virtuoso and genre-agnostic singer-songwriter (see last year's *To the Sunset*). The not-so-secret weapon is Natalie Hemby, who's made her name as an A-list Music Row writer with serious range – she co-wrote three songs on Kacey Musgraves' 2018 masterpiece, *Golden Hour,* and 10 on Miranda Lambert's landmark *The Weight of These Wings.*

Hemby's got a stoner-friendly wit that loves wordplay; see "Redesigning Women," an anthem that nods to the Eighties Southern-ladies-in-business sitcom *Designing Women,* and "My Only Child," a nuanced tear-jerker penned with Lambert and Shires that's full of sharp details ("Pink painted walls/Your face in my locket/Your daddy and me/Your tiny back pocket").

The writing's distributed equitably, and not every song goes for profundity. "Don't Call Me," a Shires co-write, is a sassy kiss-off to a leech. Morris similarly boots an unappreciative partner on "Loose Change," and joins Carlile and Shires to claim a maternal flex day on "My Name Can't Be Mama." Even the playful songs have gravity, and vice versa. "If She Ever Leaves Me," penned by Shires, husband Jason Isbell, and Chris "Before He Cheats" Tompkins, is a queer honky-tonk ballad delivered by Carlile, who advises a hot-to-trot cowboy to back off from her lover – "That's too much cologne/She likes perfume." It's plain-spoken enough to make heteronormativity seem abnormal, just as the album makes anything short of equal representation feel like both a lie and a squandered resource. ®

BRITTANY'S VIBRANT SOUL

The Alabama Shakes leader rips up tradition at the roots on an ambitious solo LP By JON DOLAN

BRITTANY HOWARD is a Southern rock & roll radical with a centuries-deep sense of history and some inspiring ideas about how to reshape it to fit our moment. As the lead singer and guitarist for the expansively retro-minded Alabama Shakes, she's combined ga-

Brittany Howard
Jaime
ATO
★★★★☆

rage rock, soul, and psychedelia. In 2015, she convened the well-named punk-rock side project Thunderbitch, reimagining vintage New York punk as roadhouse stomp.

Now, she's put the Shakes on hold to make her solo debut (though a couple of band members are on hand,

as is co-producer Shawn Everett, who engineered the Shakes' 2015 LP, *Sound & Color*). Still, it's a total departure, her kaleidoscopic mix of decades' worth of R&B, hip-hop, blues, and gospel, steeped in trippy laptop sonics and deeply personal political urgency.

"History Repeats" opens by establishing what will become a theme, sounding at once ancient and modern as it suggests a natural bridge between James Brown good-footin', "Kiss"-era Prince, and Janelle Monáe's sci-fi futurism. Howard's voice takes falsetto flight like Smokey Robinson on the Sixties soul pastorale "Stay High," and the somberly longing "Short and Sweet" recalls Nina Simone, just Howard and a soft guitar making longing feel intimate and infinite.

Howard's newest collaborators here are keyboardist Robert Glasper and drummer Nate Smith, worldly jazz musicians who help turn riffs like the cosmic boom-bap opus "13th Century Metal" into shape-shifting explorations.

The most potent moments interrogate Southern traditions in ways that go well beyond mere musical reinvention. "He Loves Me" is an anthem of lapsed religious devotion and personal freedom, sampling a black preacher who testifies about a friend who's going to live a long life "'cause he ain't worried about nothing," as Howard's guitar makes liberated noise and she praises her personal Jesus: "I know He still loves me/I know He still loves me when I'm smoking blunts."

And then there's "Georgia," a protest jam for our current right-wing apocalypse. Over a sinewy beat and a meditative organ, Howard sings a forlorn ode to a state that flagrantly depressed African American voter turnout in the 2018 election and recently passed one of the country's most egregious anti-abortion laws. Howard is mindful of Ray Charles' "Georgia on My Mind," turning its wistful nostalgia into something much sadder. "I just want Georgia to notice me," she sings, confronting oppression with faint hope. It's a strikingly bold moment on a record that's full of them. ®

FROM TOP: DANNY CLINCH; SACHA LECCA

BREAKING

Underdog Psych-Pop Heartthrob Cuco

Cuco

IN 2016, Omar Banos went viral posting a video of himself playing a slide-guitar version of Santo and Johnny's 1959 classic surf instrumental "Sleepwalk." Recording as Cuco, the SoCal native maintained that buzz by releasing psychedelia-soaked Spanglish love ballads that surprisingly struck a chord in young Latinx listeners. On his major-label debut, *Para Mí,* recorded on his sickbed after a recent car crash, he sings lines like "Take this and fly away/Till the substance numbs the pain," while proving himself a scholar of Tame Impala, Tyler the Creator, and João Gilberto. The result is a unique blend of burnout soul. **SUZY EXPOSITO**

★★★★★ Classic | ★★★★ Excellent | ★★★ Good | ★★ Fair | ★ Poor RATINGS ARE SUPERVISED BY THE EDITORS OF ROLLING STONE.

Quick Hits

Ten new albums you need to know about now

Sheer Mag
A Distant Call
Wilsuns

RADICAL RETRO The Philly band are stealth pop geniuses in the guise of street-tough rockers on their second album, able to pull off socialist punk and Fleetwood Mac-tinged beauty with equal ease and power.

★★★★☆

Muna
Saves the World
RCA

BLUE WAVE The L.A. trio's second offering is an electro-pop treat, full of rich character sketches ("It's Gonna Be OK"), self-love pep talks ("Number One Fan"), and Carly Rae Jepsen-ian romantic melancholy.

★★★★☆

Bat for Lashes
Lost Girls
Bat for Lashes

GREAT GOTH "Everything is on fire," Bat for Lashes' Natasha Khan sings, but you might not notice the flames because the music is so chilly. Few artists can make emotional crises sound so serenely beautiful.

★★★½☆

Hiss Golden Messenger
Terms of Surrender
Merge

MELLOW GOLD Seven LPs into his run as a conjurer of sunny Seventies-tinged roots rock, North Carolina's MC Taylor hits a peak, especially on somberly pretty tunes like "My Wing" and "Down at the Uptown."

★★★½☆

Iggy Pop
Free
Loma Vista

OLD POWER "Online porn is driving me nuts," the 72-year-old punk sings, proving he hasn't changed since he was a Stooge decades ago. But his music has, emphasizing jazz horns and Sinatra-esque crooning.

★★★½☆

Bon Iver
i,i
Jagjaguwar

FEEL THE VERN Justin Vernon dials back the avant-pop extremes, giving human larynxes and other acoustic instruments more flex room amid synths and Auto-Tune-y veils. It can be a brilliant balance.

★★★½☆

Pixies
Beneath the Eyrie
Infectious Music

INDIE ELDERS The tone of the alt-rock heroes' third post-reunion album is more muted than usual. But frontman Black Francis' well-sharpened melodies and sense of humor guide the band through.

★★★☆☆

Sheryl Crow
Threads
Valory

CROW AND CO. Everyone from Eric Clapton to St. Vincent appears alongside Crow on this collaborative album. The highlights are ballads with country lions Emmylou Harris and Willie Nelson.

★★★☆☆

Lumineers
III
Dualtone Music

DARKER ROOTS The Mumfords-y band gets conceptual for a song cycle about the travails of a fictional family. It's a mixed bag (see the cornball NYC homage "Life in the City"), but the moodier vibe works.

★★★☆☆

Barns Courtney
404
Capitol

LUKEWARM PLAY Rising U.K. lite rocker Courtney is like an Adderall'd Chris Martin, stacking his second LP with pummeling pop hooks and lyrical nods to acts (the Who, Prince) well beyond his pay grade.

★★½☆☆

CONTRIBUTORS: JONATHAN BERNSTEIN, JON DOLAN, KORY GROW, WILL HERMES, HANK SHTEAMER

THE GREAT INDOORS

Bedroom-pop whiz kids turn their little worlds into private utopias

"THE WORLD is crumbling and I don't have much to say," sings Greta Kline of Frankie Cosmos. But her indie-pop escapism is its own answer. The fourth Frankie Cosmos LP contains 21 precisely catchy songs built from brittle guitars, delicate hooks, and Kline's tiny, inviting voice, which rarely gets loud enough to wake a napping roommate.

Frankie Cosmos
Close It Quietly
★★★½☆

Jay Som
Anak Ko
★★★½☆

Jay Som (a.k.a. singer-guitarist Melina Duterte) does something equally sweet on her ace second album. "Superbike" radiates Eighties shoegaze glory, and "Tenderness" is snow-globe Steely Dan. The peak might be "Nighttime Drive," serene, strummy, and adorably gangster, with Duterte singing about "shoplifting at the Whole Foods." Hey, if you're going to go out into the crumbling world, might as well get yours. **JON DOLAN**

Iggy Pop

Rolling Stone GUIDE

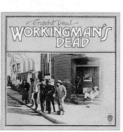

Grateful Dead

America's most expansive band – from kaleidoscopic psychedelia to homespun country rock to epic live jams and beyond

By WILL HERMES

Must-Haves

Live Dead
1969

The ultimate live document of Grateful Dead v1.0, and candidate for the best live rock album ever, is this double LP made during the distended *Aoxomoxoa*

sessions. It has the definitive reading of "Dark Star," the holy grail of Dead set lists, along with "The Eleven," a head-spinning Phil Lesh composition in 11/8 time. "Turn On Your Lovelight" is the consummate document of Ron "Pigpen" McKernan's hippie-biker R&B, and "Death Don't Have No Mercy" is Jerry Garcia at his dark-bluest.

Workingman's Dead
1970

Leaning into their love of country music and the harmonies of Crosby, Stills, Nash and Young, the Dead make the perfect Americana LP, years before the genre was coined. In a largely unplugged set, the songwriting partnership of Garcia and lyricist Robert Hunter is at its peak. "Uncle John's Band" celebrates the group's persona and community. And the cokehead cautionary tale "Casey Jones" even got them, for the first time, some significant radio play.

American Beauty
1970

The sister LP to *Workingman's Dead*, released just over four months later, rode the songwriting bonanza, with new influences digested. The result is a slightly fuller sound, a brighter vibe, and maybe, song-for-song, their strongest set ever. "Ripple" and Lesh's breakout "Box of Rain" are the Dead at their deepest, and "Sugar Magnolia" and "Truckin'," both delivered by band young'un Bob Weir, nailed the noodle-dance boogie style that took them from collegiate cult band to stadium-filling phenomenon.

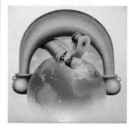

Europe '72
1972

Having perfected their stage game, the Dead take it overseas, with trusty 17-track studio in tow. The result is that rarest of things, an essential triple LP. It mixes reshaped faves (an exploded "Morning Dew," the paradigmatic melding of "China Cat Sunflower" and "I Know You Rider") with top-shelf new material ("Jack Straw," "He's Gone"), all with improvisatory fire and near-studio-quality sound. And it captures the band's shift from hard-tripping psych blues to the kinder, gentler, dancing-bear-ier music that would come to define their shows.

Further Listening

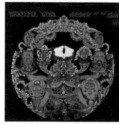

Anthem of the Sun
1968

The band's first attempt to capture its head-exploding concerts on tape resulted in this wild ride — a collage of studio and live tracks epitomized by "That's It for the Other One," a suite that's part tribute to Merry Prankster bus driver Neal Cassady. Its coda foreshadows the Beatles' "Revolution #9," and its raging center section would become a concert staple. Meanwhile, the kazoo-powered "Alligator" is a spectacular train wreck of Pigpen's earthy electric blues and his bandmates' jazzy lunar spelunking that anticipated the Allman Brothers, whose debut dropped the following year.

Aoxomoxoa
1969

Recorded after the implosion of their San Francisco scene, the peak of the Dead's experimental phase mirrored an LSD trip in miniature. Fittingly, it's a swirl of dazzling lights (side-openers "St. Stephen" and "China Cat Sunflower") and darkness (spooky denouements "Mountains of the Moon" and "What's Become of the Baby"), driven by Hunter's sly, pie-eyed poesy and a playground of cutting-edge 16-track recording landscapes. Still one of the most satisfyingly bonkers rock LPs ever made.

Grateful Dead
1971

Another live set (known alternately as Skull-Fuck and Skull and Roses), this one came with some overdubs, and furthered their tradition of introducing songs they would never bring to the studio, such as the rollicking "Bertha" and the soulful panhandler's lament "Wharf Rat." It established "The Other One" and tag-team covers like "Not Fade Away">"Goin' Down the Road Feelin' Bad" as beloved jam fulcrums. And the Kelley-Mouse art is one of the most iconic album covers in history.

Blues for Allah
1975

The Dead's muso masterpiece, perhaps their jazziest and most virtuosic set, was made during a rare hiatus from the road, at Weir's home studio. The catchiest songs are "Franklin's

Weir, Mickey Hart, Garcia, and Lesh (from left), 1968

Tower" (whose central riff may or may not be an intentional echo of the signature "doo-doo-doo" reprise on Lou Reed's "Walk on the Wild Side") and "The Music Never Stopped," a funky strut with duet vocals by new band member Donna Jean Godchaux. But half the fun is the LP's spate of instrumentals: the curlicue speed trial "King Solomon's Marbles," the twining "Help on the Way" coda "Slipknot!" and the pastoral "Sage & Spirit."

Terrapin Station
1977

Veteran hitmaker Clive Davis signed the Dead to his Arista label, and this was the first fruit: a polished LP built on a sidelong title suite, an epic fireside tale penned by Hunter and crooned sweetly by Garcia, and buoyed by the Aaron Copland-esque orchestrations of Paul Buckmaster and gleaming production by Fleetwood Mac wingman Keith Olsen. Even Garcia's guitar morphed, via burbling envelope-filter effects, on "Estimated Prophet," a sound that would become a latter-day staple.

Going Deeper

Grateful Dead
1967

At their label's behest, the Dead cut their debut at RCA Studios in Hollywood, instead of their San Francisco home base, and the result was a set of electrified folk-blues covers that suggest a band gulping amphetamines. (They were.) Standouts are a roaring reboot of the 1930 Mississippi Sheiks single "Sitting on Top of the World"; the soon-to-be-signature cover of "Cold Rain and Snow"; a 10-minute unpacking of Gus Cannon's 1928 disc

MICHAEL PUTLAND/GETTY IMAGES

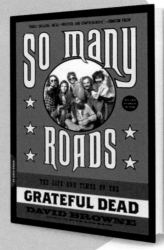

So Many Roads: The Life and Times of the Grateful Dead By David Browne

This authoritative book by ROLLING STONE senior writer Browne brings the band's epic story into the 21st century with a vivid narrative rooted in specific gigs, where the heart of the band's story ultimately resides. For an insider's account, see *Long Strange Trip,* by the band's publicist Dennis McNally.

"Viola Lee Blues"; and a couple of almost-there originals: "Cream Puff War" and "The Golden Road (To Unlimited Devotion)."

Wake of the Flood
1973

The band's self-produced debut release on its own label is laid-back, occasionally to a fault. But the songs are largely primo, many already concert highlights. Foremost is the dilated dance-jam supreme "Eyes of the World." Runners-up: "Mississippi Half Step Uptown Toodeloo," with Vassar Clements' swinging hot-club fiddle, and the exquisite stoner-philosophical reverie "Stella Blue," namesake of innumerable boats, bars, and puppies.

From the Mars Hotel
1974

Unusual for not one but two songs written and sung by bass magician/AWOL classical-music student Lesh — the woozy "Unbroken Chain," with its spaceships-landing synths, and the swaggering "Pride of

Cucamonga." Skirt-twirling fave "Scarlet Begonias" would be the keeper. Other highlights: the post-Watergate "U.S. Blues," which still feels timely, and the shade-throwing "Ship of Fools," soulfully covered years later by Elvis Costello.

In the Dark
1987

The Dead's Arista deal was in part a band-endorsed attempt to "sell out." They succeeded with the irresistibly avuncular "Touch of Grey." The writing is solid throughout, with the Hunter-Garcia ballad "Black Muddy River" being the downtempo standout. It channels a recurring nightmare of Hunter's with a tapestry of Dead symbology: mountains, moons, stars, sunshine, ripples, and "the last rose of summer."

Cornell 5/8/77
2017

The various Dead archival series — including *Dick's Picks, Dave's Picks,* and *From the Vault* — are a universe unto themselves. On the basis of a widely circulated bootleg, this midlife show in Ithaca, New York, was for years considered by some the greatest-ever Dead concert. That standing is debatable, but there's no arguing with the immolative "Scarlet Begonias">"Fire on the Mountain," or the phoenix-rising majesty of "Morning Dew."

Loose Joints

Highlights from the rest of the band's massive catalog

"BIRD SONG"
Garcia, 1972
This eulogy for Janis Joplin on Garcia's debut solo LP doesn't feature the full band. But it would become a gorgeous staple of Dead sets henceforth.

"PLAYING IN THE BAND"
Ace, 1972
Weir's solo debut is a Dead LP in all but name, and this would be a familiar second set jam-launchpad for the rest of the band's career.

"HARD TO HANDLE"
The History of the Grateful Dead, Vol. One (Bear's Choice), 1973
A roaring Otis Redding cover delivered by Pigpen, recorded live in 1970 and released on this tribute-of-sorts to the singer-keyboardist, who died in 1973.

"STELLA BLUE"
Steal Your Face, 1976
An aching, eight-minute-plus live reading of this ruefully ruminative *Wake of the Flood* gem.

"SHAKEDOWN STREET"
Shakedown Street, 1978
The pinnacle of what fans and critics alike dubbed "disco Dead," aided by crisp production by Little Feat linchpin Lowell George.

"ALL ALONG THE WATCHTOWER"
Dylan & the Dead, 1985
The highlight of an inexplicably pale document of this marvelous curveball tour.

"MASON'S CHILDREN"
So Many Roads, 1999
This outtake from the *Workingman's Dead* sessions alludes obliquely to the horror show of Altamont, according to Hunter.

"STANDING ON THE MOON"
Built to Last, 1989
A weary blues about the follies of man, and with specific references to Southeast Asia and El Salvador; one of the band's more political songs.

"DAYS BETWEEN"
Los Angeles Sports Arena, 12/19/94, archive.org
The last Garcia-Hunter masterpiece: a dark, gorgeous meditation on life's arc.

Garcia in London, 1972

T.V.

David Simon's Vision of America

More than a decade after *The Wire*, Simon proves he's still one of the edgiest and most dynamic showrunners in the game By ALAN SEPINWALL

HBO'S FIRST golden age had its holy trinity of Davids: *The Sopranos'* David Chase, *Deadwood's* David Milch, and *The Wire's* David Simon. In the years since, Chase and Milch receded before returning to their old favorites – Chase with a *Sopranos* prequel, Milch with a *Deadwood* reunion. Simon, though, has no interest in reviving *The Wire*. He already told that story. Besides, HBO has kept him busy since the day we said goodbye to his fictionalized Baltimore: first with the Iraq War miniseries *Generation Kill*, then the post-Katrina drama *Treme*, the political miniseries *Show Me a Hero*, and the porn drama *The Deuce*, which begins its third and final season on September 9th.

The Wire, little-watched when it originally aired, is now often hailed as the greatest show ever made. Its combination of gripping police stories and blunt talk about failing American institutions made it the ultimate televised example of a spoonful of sugar making the medicine go down. A converted journalist, Simon is a great pure storyteller who manages to invest nearly every character with startling depth. But he's long pushed back against people who dwell on the most popcorn aspects of his masterpiece. Perhaps not coincidentally, his post-*Wire* projects have been less commercial.

Treme often felt like one of the jazz compositions its trombonist hero, Antoine Batiste (Wendell Pierce), hustled around New Orleans to play: lively but amorphous. There were some clear narrative signposts, but *Treme* mostly provided a chance to marinate in the atmosphere of a great American city and the show's superb ensemble.

Generation Kill, about the '03 Iraq invasion, was also intentionally chaotic – the better to reflect what its Marine protagonists experienced during a hastily conceived military action. Large swaths of it turn into dark road-trip comedy, until the adventure fizzles out, because no one in charge has a plan for what to do after Iraqi forces have been steamrolled.

The public-housing premise of *Show Me a Hero* almost sounds like a parody of a Simon project. But if it's wonky, it's also as compulsively watchable as anything he's made. It's Simon's first time working with a famous director (*Crash's* Paul Haggis), and with pre-existing stars like Oscar Isaac and Catherine Keener, rather than ones he created, like Idris Elba and Michael B. Jordan.

The Deuce in many ways feels like a culmination of everything Simon's done since saying goodbye to McNulty and Omar. Like *Show Me a Hero*, it has high-profile leads in Maggie Gyllenhaal (as a prostitute turned feminist porn auteur) and James Franco (as identical twins caught up in vice to varying degrees). Like

THE MOST BANG FOR YOUR TV BUCK
From *Treme* to *Generation Kill*, *Show Me a Hero*, and *The Deuce*, all of Simon's shows in the 11 years post-*Wire* have been masterworks of high-wattage entertainment that double as engaging civics lessons.

Treme, its strongest appeal is its sense of place (the grimy pre-Giuliani Times Square). And like *Generation Kill*, it's a period piece about grand plans for which no one has considered the unintended consequences. It's sometimes too sprawling for its own good, but still a potent reminder that Simon and his collaborators can be as good at pure entertainment as they are at dramatizing civics lessons.

This final season jumps into the mid-Eighties. Director Harvey (David Krumholtz) tells Gyllenhaal's Candy they have to abandon their loftier artistic impulses to make money in this new home-video market, and calls her films "a niche product that I can no longer invest in." It's hard not to view their arguments as Simon and co-creator George Pelecanos reckoning with their position as art-house filmmakers at a network that, thanks to *Game of Thrones* and corporate mergers, is looking for blockbusters. But Simon hasn't been coasting on reputation in the 11 years since his masterpiece ended. His shows still feel vital, relevant, and often shockingly fun. So he hasn't made *The Wire 2: Wire Harder* yet. So what? His stuff's still all in the game. ⓡ

ILLUSTRATION BY **Nazario Graziano**

WATCH LIST

What to stream, what to skip this month

D'Onofrio, Whitaker square off.

FIGHT THE POWER

Godfather of Harlem

NETWORK	Epix
AIR DATE	September 29th

★★★☆☆

"I got guns," legendary gangster Bumpy Johnson (Forest Whitaker) announces. "I got soldiers," Malcolm X (Nigel Thatch) replies. It's a match made in gritty-drama heaven in this Sixties period piece that mixes Mob action with civil-rights rhetoric. The cast is stacked: Giancarlo Esposito is Congressman Adam Clayton Powell Jr.; Vincent D'Onofrio, Paul Sorvino, and Chazz Palminteri are infamous Mafioso with limited tolerance for Johnson's activities. ("You know that nobody likes you people getting all loud and boisterous, right?" D'Onofrio's gangster sneers.)

Everyone's wildly overqualified for the material, which feels like *Boardwalk Empire* minus the artier pretensions. But the music — a mix of period tunes and original hip-hop, curated by Swizz Beatz — is great, and Whitaker gets to unleash his remarkable onscreen temper long enough to create the illusion that this *Godfather* is worthy of that name.

CASHING OUT

On Becoming a God in Central Florida

NETWORK	Showtime
AIR DATE	Sundays, 10 p.m.

★★½☆☆

In an early episode of this dramedy about American delusions, Kirsten Dunst's Krystal is greeted by her husband's pyramid-scheme boss, Cody (Théodore Pellerin), who offers her a cookie cake and a creepy, painted-on smile to make her feel better about the scam obliterating her life savings. Once upon a time, Dunst would have nailed playing a falsely chipper zombie like Cody. *On Becoming a God in Central Florida* smartly turns her fundamental sunniness on its head. Krystal has no patience for Cody's bullshit and responds to him with a perfect expression of disdain.

Dunst is wonderful, and the show makes some strong satirical points early on about the lies we are conditioned to tell ourselves in order to pursue the fortunes to which we are allegedly entitled. But it quickly runs out of things to say, leaving us to spend way too much time in the company of the pyramid scheme's acolytes and its leader (Ted Levine). As a two-hour movie, this story would run out of

Dunst sells her soul.

steam too quickly. As a 10-episode series, it becomes as exhausting to sit through as Krystal finds Cody. Her contempt for the whole enterprise, and the sharp edges of Dunst's performance, cut through some of this unpleasant cult's inanity, but not enough. There's a scene of black-comic violence in the premiere that's hilarious for its surprise; by the time the finale strikes a similar note, the show feels too labored for anything to be funny.

TRUTH BE TOLD

Unbelievable

NETWORK	Netflix
AIR DATE	September 13th

★★★★☆

Wever (left), Collette

This miniseries about sexual assault and the trauma that reverberates around it is essentially two different shows operating under one title. In the first, *Booksmart*'s Kaitlyn Dever is a young woman who reports her assault, then recants under pressure from skeptical cops, and is charged with filing a false report. In the second, cops Toni Collette and Merritt Wever team up to pursue a serial rapist. The detectives are clearly chasing Dever's attacker, but the stories mostly stay on parallel tracks: one an emotionally brutal tale of a woman victimized first by a rapist, then by the system; the other a thoughtful but also propulsive police procedural.

Both halves are superb, as are the leads (particularly Wever), but the police story is the easier one to get through. The show devotes the entire first episode to Dever's horrifying situation, which might scare away viewers unwilling to endure seven more hours like it. Be patient: *Unbelievable* offers ample rewards. **A.S.**

★★★★★ Classic | ★★★★ Excellent | ★★★ Good | ★★ Fair | ★ Poor

CLOCKWISE FROM TOP: DAVID LEE/EPIX; BETH DUBBER/NETFLIX; PATRICK MCELHENNEY/FXX; PATTI PERRET/SONY/SHOWTIME

The 'Sunny' Side of Life

As *It's Always Sunny in Philadelphia* returns for a history-making 14th season, creator and co-star Rob McElhenney explains the keys to the black comedy's against-all-odds longevity.

WHEN "IT'S ALWAYS Sunny in Philadelphia" returns to FXX on September 25th, it'll tie *The Adventures of Ozzie and Harriet* as the longest-running live-action comedy in American TV history. How has this scruffy DIY sitcom about a group of pals (a.k.a. "the Gang") arguing about abortion, sexual harassment, drug addiction, and more lasted this long — and been so consistently, scathingly funny? By sticking with what works.

The formula is simple: A hot-button topic comes up; the Gang has the worst possible response to it; repeat. But as *Sunny* creator and star Rob McElhenney says, "Because the world seems to change so much from a cultural perspective, each year gives us a bunch of new cultural things that have changed that we can mine."

That the Gang are all sociopaths (and Glenn Howerton's Dennis may be a serial killer) has actually helped in the long run. The fact that these people never grow up just provides more comic fodder. "The older it gets," says McElhenney, "the sadder it gets, the funnier it gets."

As for Season 14? "It's more of the same!" he promises. "Hopefully there are episodes that'll satisfy people who like the show, and will also enrage some people. Part of my job is subverting the expectation of my core base on a consistent basis. They might have to watch a four-and-a-half-minute contemporary-dance sequence. They might scream at the TV in rage. But I promise them that is why they like the show: They don't know what's coming." **A.S.**

McElhenney and Danny DeVito

Movies

The contenders (clockwise from top): Ridley battles in *Star Wars: The Rise of Skywalker*; Pacino, De Niro are hoods in *The Irishman*; Bale and Damon build a dynasty in *Ford v Ferrari*.

14 MUST-SEES FOR FALL

From a Jedi to a Joker, gangsters to speed freaks, popcorn films hunt for awards

PETER TRAVERS

Ad Astra
September 20th

Brad Pitt blasts off as an astronaut in search of his lost flyboy dad (Tommy Lee Jones). Nothing like starting the fall on a dare: Director/co-writer James Gray describes his sci-fi head trip as "the most realistic depiction of space travel that's been put in a movie." Since Gray is a renegade indie master (*The Yards, Two Lovers, The Lost City of Z*) not given to idle brags, better buckle up.

Joker
October 4th

So you think Heath Ledger's 2008 take on the DC Comics villain in *The Dark Knight* is unbeatable? (Hell, he won a posthumous Oscar.) Just wait till you get a load of Joaquin Phoenix, who reinvents the role as a failed stand-up comic who decides to pass himself off as Crime's Clown Prince. Neither Ledger, Jack Nicholson (in 1989's *Batman*), nor Jared Leto (2016's *Suicide Squad*) has ever played Joker as a starring role. Anyone doubt that Phoenix has the mad skills to take things to the limit?

Gemini Man
October 11th

Will Smith plays a hitman about to be retired by a younger version of himself, also played by Smith, looking like he just stepped off the set of *The Fresh Prince of Bel-Air.* If the plot rings with echoes of 2012's *Looper,* trust director Ang Lee to show how far computers can come to matching God's work with humans. Game on.

Smith

Jojo Rabbit
October 18th

Taika Waititi, the visionary New Zealander who sparked such inspired lunacy with Chris Hemsworth in *Thor: Ragnarok,* wrote and directed this ink-dark World War II comedy that throws away the rules. Roman Griffin Davis is Jojo, a bullied German boy who conjures an imaginary friend in a cuckoo version of Adolf Hitler, played by Waititi himself. Those not offended will laugh helplessly.

Terminator: Dark Fate
November 1st

It's a reunion for *Terminator* fans. Producer James Cameron says *Dark Fate* (*T6*) is a direct follow-up to his 1984 *T1* and 1991 *T2* – so much for the three in-betweeners. That means Ah-nuld is back as T-800, along with Linda Hamilton as Sarah Connor and Edward Furlong as her son, John. Resistance is futile.

Motherless Brooklyn
November 1st

Edward Norton triumphantly fulfills his passion project to write, produce, direct, and star in the film version of Jonathan Lethem's acclaimed novel about a Brooklyn detective who has Tourette's syndrome.

Ford v Ferrari
November 15th

Director James Mangold powers this speeding drama, set in 1966, when the Ford Motor Company tried to end Enzo Ferrari's dominance at Le Mans. Matt Damon as Ford design whiz Carroll Shelby and Christian Bale as the turbulent British driver Ken Miles should whoosh the film into the awards race.

Phoenix reinvents an icon in *Joker*.

★★★★★ Classic | ★★★★ Excellent | ★★★ Good | ★★ Fair | ★ Poor

The Irishman
Date TBD

It's unlikely that any film this fall can top this epic crime saga from Martin Scorsese, reunited for the ninth time with Robert De Niro and directing Al Pacino for the first time. De Niro plays Frank Sheeran, the hitman linked to the disappearance of labor leader Jimmy Hoffa (Pacino). The digital de-aging of the actors, including Scorsese regular Joe Pesci, helped balloon the film's cost past $200 million. But with these titans playing goodfellas through the decades, expect history in the making.

A Beautiful Day in the Neighborhood
November 22nd

Mr. Nice Guy Tom Hanks portrays Fred Rogers, the beloved Mr. Nice Guy of preschool TV programming.

Johansson, Robertson, Driver

Where's the tension? It's in the script, based on an *Esquire* article by Tom Junod, in which a skeptical journalist, played by Matthew Rhys (an Emmy winner for *The Americans*), attempts a deep-dive probe into the gentle creator and host of *Mister Rogers' Neighborhood*. From Hanks and skilled director Marielle Heller (*Can You Ever Forgive Me?*), expect the unexpected.

Uncut Gems
December 13th

Josh and Benny Safdie follow up their sensational *Good Time* with another crime caper laced with mirth and malice. *Uncut Gems* stars Adam Sandler, proving again that when he wants to, he can act with the best of them. Sandler plays a Manhattan jeweler who freaks when diamonds go missing, sparking cinematic anarchy only the Safdies can deliver.

Star Wars: The Rise of Skywalker
December 20th

It's here – the final episode of the nine-part Skywalker saga. No spoilers, but Daisy Ridley is back as Rey, the last known Jedi, in fierce resistance to Kylo Ren (Adam Driver), the Supreme Leader of the First Order. Will director J.J. Abrams (*The Force Awakens*) reunite the whole gang for the fade-out? May the Force be with tradition.

Marriage Story
Date TBD

Noah Baumbach's best film yet concerns the breakup of a New York theater director (Adam Driver) and his actress wife (Scarlett Johansson). Can they divorce and yet survive as parents to their son (Azhy Robertson)? Sublime performances, and let's just say it: Driver is one of the finest actors on the planet.

Little Women
December 25th

What happens when Greta Gerwig, the Oscar-touted creator of *Lady Bird,* tackles the eighth film of Louisa May Alcott's 1868 novel? Will the young lives of the March sisters – Jo (Saoirse Ronan), Meg (Emma Watson), and Amy (Florence Pugh) – speak to our current moment?

1917
December 25th

Set in the depths of World War I, this epic from *Skyfall* director Sam Mendes puts two Brit soldiers (George MacKay and Dean-Charles Chapman) on a suicide mission. Producer Steven Spielberg calls *1917* "hugely daring and ambitious." So are all the top fall films. But who gets the Oscar gold? ®

Sandler shines.

'IT' BY THE NUMBERS

Total copies in *It*'s first printing:
800,000

Number of Stephen King books sold overall:
350 million

Rating for *It* — the two-part 1990 TV miniseries:
36.7 million households

Box-office gross of *It* (2017) on opening weekend:
$123 million

Box office gross of *It* (2017) worldwide:
$700 million

It boy: Pennywise reflects.

HORROR

'It: Chapter Two' — In Praise of Pennywise

Stephen King's most terrifying character is at his nightmare-inducing, all-time best By DAVID FEAR

IN A NUTSHELL, *It: Chapter Two* is a better movie than the first one. The upgrade to the adult version of the "Losers Club" – now played by Jessica Chastain, Bill Hader, James McAvoy, and others – makes the story feel less like a faded copy of other films and TV shows that have cannibalized Stephen King's work in the name of homage (looking at you, *Stranger Things*). It's as much about trauma, healing, and making peace with your past as it is about jump scares. The ending is . . . well, it's the book's ending, which, *yeesh*. And the clown? The clown is even more terrifying this time around. Seriously.

When King conceived *It,* he admitted that the idea was to write an epic book featuring, in his words, "all of the monsters." The vampire, the werewolf, the mummy – the entire stable of vintage-horror, bump-in-the-night fodder. But he needed one character outside this old creature-feature canon, something that would inspire a sense of fear and revulsion on sight. "What scares kids the most?" he asked himself. Thus was born Pennywise, circus-centric chomper of children, destroyer of innocence, the most name-recognizable King creation this side of Cujo, and the single most horrifying nightmare the author ever dreamed up. The monster-mash idea quickly went away. Who needs Frankenstein's monster when you have a fucked-up clown?

And with all due respect to Tim Curry, whose portrayal of Pennywise in the 1990 TV miniseries scarred a generation, it's Swedish actor Bill Skarsgård's interpretation of this fright-haired bogeyman that has made the character iconic. His introduction as a voice and a pair of glowing eyes beckoning a little boy to come closer, closer, *closer* to a sewer grate channeled the book's mix of *Grimm's Fairy Tale* and gross-out horror flick. Now, in *Chapter Two*, we get an even more off-the-leash Pennywise from him, one that ups the drooling and the singsong voice and the rancid, perverse giggling. When he lures a little girl into his trap under the bleachers, you see Skarsgård go from dopey to dreamlike to slightly demented, before finding the predatory sweet spot of sympathetic vulnerability. Then out spring the fangs, and you see every childhood nightmare come to life.

King's greatest works have always revolved around finding a primal-fear button and brutally mashing it, and Pennywise was his phobic masterpiece in pancake makeup. On the page, he read like a precisely pitched blend of Freddie Krueger and Ronald McDonald. Onscreen, he feels like he's burrowing into your psyche. "There were points where I felt like I was going insane," Skarsgård said after playing the role the first time. For Round Two, he succeeds in making viewers feel *they're* going insane – which makes him the perfect King nightmare for 2019. Accept no psycho-clown substitutes. ®

Books.

TA-NEHISI COATES' AMERICAN ODYSSEY

The author of 'Between the World and Me' explores the burden of slavery from the inside with his masterful debut novel By DAVID FEAR

TA-NEHISI Coates is the most important essayist in a generation and a writer who changed the national political conversation about race with his 2015 memoir, *Between the World and Me.* So naturally his debut novel comes with slightly unrealistic expectations – and then proceeds to exceed them. *The Water Dancer,* Coates' meditation on the legacy of slavery, is a work of both staggering imagination and rich historical significance.

The novel opens with two men crashing a horse-drawn carriage into the Goose River in mid-1800s Virginia. One man drowns; the other finds himself enveloped in a blue mist and then jolted awake miles away, dazed and confused and unharmed. The man who emerges from that would-be watery grave is Hiram Walker, a slave, the product of a white master's rape and the servant to his wastrel half-brother. Those forced to give their bodies, their free will, and their lives on Hiram's father's plantations are known as "the Tasked." Their owners, the aristocrats of the antebellum South, are "the Quality."

Hiram is a little different from the rest of the Tasked, however. He has a photographic memory, which earns him privileges, if not full personhood, among the gentry. And in a supernatural twist, he

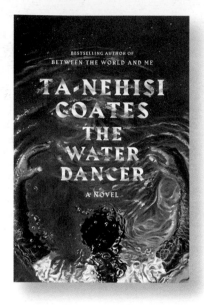

The Water Dancer

Ta-Nehisi Coates

ONE WORLD

★★★★⯪

also possesses the extraordinary gift of "conduction" – an ability to move through space and time. There's talk of another person up north who has the same talent, a woman they call the "Moses" of the Underground Railroad. And when Hiram attempts to escape Virginia, he'll eventually find himself recruited to use his conductive powers for a vast abolitionist network that will eventually take him in search of answers, a loved one, and maybe even a way to liberate his people.

Coates re-creates the world of the pre-Civil War South – from the plantations' cramped slave quarters and ornate parlors to abolitionist gatherings to the jails run by Southern militias – with a journalist's eye and ear for detail. His years as a contributor at *The Atlantic* and other publications have paid off; so has his tenure writing the Marvel comic *Black Panther,* given the way he invests his narrative with a compelling forward momentum.

What's most powerful is the way Coates enlists his notions of the fantastic, as well as his fluid prose, to probe a wound that never seems to heal. "To forget is to truly slave," one character says. "To forget is to truly die." There's an urgency to his remembrance of things past that brims with authenticity, testifying to centuries of bone-deep pain. It makes *The Water Dancer* feel timeless and instantly canon-worthy.

DEEP LISTENING

Untangling the Threads of the Trump-Russia Scandal

Putin and Trump, 2017

The Asset

Center for American Progress

★★★★☆

It's hard to keep up with a story like Donald Trump and Russia — especially since the audiobook of the Mueller report works better as an Ambien alternative than as an informative listen. So it's a good thing we have *The Asset,* a new podcast on the scandal, hosted by Max Bergmann, who served in the State Department from 2011 to 2017. Bergmann has the natural ease of someone explaining foreign policy over dinner so that the information sticks. He gets into Trump's shady business past, Vladimir Putin's rise in the KGB, and how Trump's ego made him a perfect mark. By the time it's over, you'll have only one question left: How do we get out of this mess? **ELISABETH GARBER-PAUL**

How Tegan & Sara Found Their Voice

TWIN SISTER indie-pop duo Tegan and Sara's debut memoir is a lot like their songs: complexly intimate, smartly crafted, and packing a subtle emotional wallop. The pair co-wrote *High School,* alternating authorship between chapters and focusing exclusively on

High School

Tegan and Sara

MCD

★★★★☆

their teenage years as they map out their symbiotic coming-of-age chaos. "There is...great comfort that comes from traveling through life with a witness," Tegan writes. They grew up in Calgary, Alberta, during the mid-Nineties, fighting like Ray and Dave Davies, worshipping Nirvana, and going to raves and punk shows. One day, they come across their mom's boyfriend's guitar in a storage nook ("The weight of the wood felt intimate, touching almost all of me at once," Sara writes). They start writing songs, and eventually win a local battle-of-the-bands that leads to a record deal. The emotions that fuel those songs echo their experience falling for girls and struggling with worries about being judged by the people around them. Some of the book's most heartbreaking moments come as they navigate a tense space where friendships end and relationships might begin. "There could be nothing worse than being called a lesbian," Sara writes. "Especially if you were one." What emerges is a quietly heroic origin story. **JON DOLAN**

FAMOUS

FALL FAVORITES |2019|

THE GOOD STUFF BOTANICALS

This Hemp Cream is Dermatologist Approved ➤

Made with Certified Organic sustainable ingredients and mineral water from a hot spring, Gypsy Cream has replaced the use of a steroid cream in hospitals. Try it on psoriasis, eczema, dermatitis, rosacea and dry skin!

Use Code: 20RS for 20% Off!

thegoodstuffbotanicals.com

‹enso RINGS

Premium Silicone Rings infused with precious elements. Show your commitment without sacrificing fashion or function.

www.ensorings.com

NOMAD

‹ The Perfect Wireless Charger

With 3 high-power charging coils and a built-in Apple Watch charger, Base Station Apple Watch creates a frictionless charging experience.

www.hellonomad.com

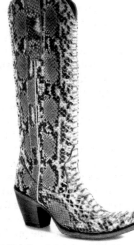

Fight Inflammation Deliciously! ➤

Turmeric, Ginger, Tart Cherries & more! 100% natural protein bars promote relief from inflammation associated with exercise.

12g protein. Gluten-free. High fiber.

10% off with code RS10

NIRVANABARS.com

HANDCRAFTED CORRAL BOOTS

Established in Texas, USA. ➤ Corral boots brand has been handcrafting high-quality fashion Cowgirl boots since 1998 for a fair price.

www.corralboots.com

‹ Wahl Beard Care Line

Men with worship-worthy whiskers know the best beards aren't born — they're made. It takes patience, care and Wahl's new line of beard products.

WahlUSA.com

‹ Styling Curly Hair?

Mixed Chicks has been taming frizz and defining multicultural curls since 2004...all hair types.

Available at grocery stores and retail chains near you. *If not, ask your store to carry us. :)*

MixedChicks.net

MDR® Vital Factors® ➤

Revitalize Youthful Energy. Support brain function, muscle tone, and immunity. Enjoy greater vitality and peak performance. Optimize your health with this anti-aging nutritional formula packed with HGH profactors, Resveratrol, and Antioxidants.

As seen on TV. Results Guaranteed!

Special: 10 Effervescent Tabs - just $15!

VitalFactors.tv | Amazon.com

or call 800.637.8227

LASER HAIR REMOVAL - IN A TUBE! ➤

End the misery of unwanted hair with this new discovery from Japan. Hairfree kills the root - just like laser hair removal - for a fraction of the cost! Permanently gets rid of thick hair growth on men. No more shaving, plucking, waxing. Safe and natural. Works for all hair colors. For men & women.

60 day money-back guarantee. **ORDER ONLINE NOW!**

$10 off & free shipping with Promo Code: TR23

www.hair-free-hair-remover.com

⌂ date NIGHT IN BOXES

‹ Date night from the comfort of your home.
No planning required!

With this custom-created, date night subscription experience, create everlasting memories through meaningful conversation and creative activities.

Get 15% off with code: DNISTONE

www.nightinboxes.com

‹LectroFan micro2

‹ Travel's better when you're well rested.

Hit the road with this compact and colorful Bluetooth speaker and sleep sound machine.

www.soundofsleep.com

1.866.220.7607

H2O Media inc. | h2omediainc.com | info@h2omediainc.com

→ HOUSING CRISIS

[*Cont. from 55*] support grew from 61 percent to 66 percent, he says. "Support in every region of the state, every demographic, including older white people, including homeowners – everyone."

Portantino says it was a "jolt" to cities that have failed to act. "I do think now everybody's going to come to the table, and I'm getting optimistic about finding the sweet spot," he says. But it will take a herculean effort, and perhaps more involvement from Gov. Newsom. Despite his promise to build 3.5 million new houses, approvals for construction are down 12 percent in 2019, and Newsom was largely absent from the debate over SB50. ("The governor continues to believe California can and must do more to address the housing shortage and the high cost of housing and rent, and he will continue working with the Legislature to do just that," Newsom's press secretary said in a statement, adding that Newsom approved a budget with $1.75 billion to jump-start construction and allocated "more state money than ever" to fight homelessness.) "He said all the right things, gave all the indications that this was his top priority, and then he just disappeared," Shaw says of the governor. "He's invisible."

SB50 WAS NOT the only legislation that disappointed advocates this year, only the most high-profile. In May, almost all the major housing bills proposed (there were more than 200 total) went up in flames. Two renter-protection bills were killed, and a third, to shield against egregious rent increases, passed only after it was effectively gutted. A tax credit benefiting the owners of historic or architecturally significant homes, "such as the craftsman, the California ranch, the mission revival & art deco building," sailed through the chamber, however.

The best that Democrats are able to offer the homeless is the creation of more safe parking lots. AB891, one of a number of parking-lot bills still alive in the Legislature, would require every California city with a population greater than 330,000 to establish a parking program like the one in San Jose.

"It's not a solution," says Jen Loving, an advocate for the homeless who works with the city of San Jose. "Anything that is not solving homelessness – providing an affordable place for someone to live – is an interim measure.... Shelters, safe parking, temporary stuff is providing more safety for people than they might have out on the streets on their own, but we're not ending homelessness that way – ending homelessness in the state of California requires political courage at the state and local levels."

Until the state's politicians find the courage to act, families like Adelle Amador's will be stuck living in their cars. "It's a test for us," Amador says. "We're going to make it through or we're not. I think we're going to.... I got a lot of faith."

For as little as it offers, she still sees the parking lot as progress. "Believe me, five years ago they weren't offering all this stuff," she says. "There was none of this help. At times, me and my husband felt like we were the only ones out here with our kids. My kids been out here for so long. All they ever want is just a home. That's all I ever hear them going, 'I just want a home.' "I'm like, 'I know, guys. I know it's going to happen.' Believe me, I got a lot of faith in my heart, and I know it's going to happen for us." ®

→ EXTREME HEAT

[*Cont. from 83*] Heitz offers her a couple of bottles of water, which she takes, stockpiling them beside her.

As we walk back to the van, Heitz says this summer will be brutal for her and for all of the homeless in the city. "If you're smart, you figure out ways to survive, to adapt," he says. "You find friends with cool houses where you can crash during the day. You learn which churches are open."

But not everyone is so wise. Heitz tells me about a man he found lying in the heat on the sidewalk. His face was flushed, his eyes were dilated, and he wasn't moving. "I called 911, and they took him to the hospital," Heitz says. "The guy was cooking right there on the sidewalk."

In Phoenix, the brutality of life beyond the halo of air conditioning was evident everywhere I went. A few days after my visit with Heitz, I pull my rental car over to answer some emails near the corner of Indian School Road and Central Avenue. It is a nothing place, just a big intersection where 12 lanes of traffic cross. There are a few palm trees and a concrete sidewalk and some nondescript buildings that look like microprocessors on a giant PC board. I could feel the heat radiating off the asphalt and concrete as if I were standing beside a blast furnace. It was as inhuman and inhospitable a spot on this planet as anywhere I've ever been.

It doesn't have to be that way. You can build a city on a human scale, and in such a way that it does not cook people who can't afford an iced latte at Starbucks. You can power the world without fossil fuels and stop the buildup of CO_2 in the atmosphere. But so far, we haven't. The sprawl in Phoenix, as in most cities, continues unabated. And until that changes, so too will the heat.

As I fiddle with my phone, I notice a woman pacing the sidewalk ahead of me. She is rail-thin. In her skin, I see years of sun. I assume she is homeless, but maybe not. She approaches the passenger-side window of my car. There is fear in her eyes.

I roll down the window.

"I'm looking for my father," she says quickly. "Have you seen him?" She describes him and says he is supposed to meet her here every Thursday. She says he is 56 years old and doesn't have a place to stay and she is worried about him.

I tell her I haven't seen him, that I was just driving by.

"I want to find him before it gets fucking hot," she says. "I need to get out of this city. I'm like a bird, you know. I migrate. But I don't want to leave until I find my father."

She is jittery. She asks me again if I have seen her father, and I tell her I have not. Then she just turns and continues pacing along the sidewalk.

I thought of her a few days later as the temperature in Phoenix soared past 100°F. The Maricopa County Department of Public Health reported its first heat-related death of 2019: A homeless man had been found dead in a vehicle near downtown. No name or other details were released. I wondered if it might have been that woman's lost father, but I knew it was unlikely. Still, the worst of the summer heat hadn't arrived yet, and as the temperatures rise in Phoenix and cities around the world, superheated by the civilized world's insatiable appetite for fossil fuels, there are so many deaths to come. ®

[*Cont. from 67*] Weezer got their name during Cuomo's phone call with the booker that day, from a nickname Cuomo's biological father gave him. His dad wasn't in his life much after his parents' divorce, when he was four years old or so, and he had strong, unresolved feelings about it all. He had already used the name "Weezer" as a label from one of his cassettes of new songs. "I remember getting letters from my dad and it would always be, 'To Weezer.' He didn't use an 'h,'" says Cuomo. "It was definitely a very emotional name for me – and I don't think for anyone else. For the other guys in the band, it's just a weird word. I guess it even ties back to what I was saying about 'Sliver.' Just this feeling of being this helpless little kid that's abandoned, or neglected. It was definitely the right name."

That night, they played a club that had been filled with beautiful young women who had lined up to see Reeves, a heartthrob then and now. "Dogstar played and played and played," Cropper says. "They finished, and all the pretty girls went away. Five or so people who were our friends stayed. But we left it all on the stage."

WEEZER SPENT A good chunk of 1992 playing shows to mostly empty clubs with the same group of five or so friends cheering them on. Sharp started asking them not to come, on the grounds that they were bumming him out. The increasingly hive-minded Sharp and Cuomo were sharing an apartment, and Wilson and Cropper were not invited to join them. Wilson was, by his own description, "a slob" and "annoying." He ended up living in a garage with no running water. "I shit in a bag," he reveals, with a hint of pride. "Because I had to go! And there was nowhere to go. And I'm convinced the gods of rock said, 'That kid's a true believer. We've got to put the thumb on the scale for the old Weeze.'"

In November, they recorded a demo that included a version of the confessional "Say It Ain't So" that made its John Frusciante influence a lot more obvious than the one they'd lay down in the studio. The demo made it to Todd Sullivan, an A&R guy at Geffen, which became the one major label to show interest in Weezer (an indie, Slash Records, also chased them) – though he had trouble grokking them down at first, comparing their demo to the Ramones and the Descendents, as well as the Pixies, and coming away from a live show wondering if they were British.

Weezer signed to Geffen for a modest deal, and Sharp and Cuomo had every intention of producing an album themselves. Sullivan convinced them otherwise. He recalls that Paul Kolderie and Sean Slade, who produced Dinosaur Jr. and Radiohead's *Pablo Honey,* were interested, but Cuomo had been listening to the Cars' *Greatest Hits,* and became excited at the idea of Ric Ocasek, who liked what he heard. "Their demo was just a thick slab of mud with some music mixed in," says Ocasek, who was fully won over after sitting through a band rehearsal. "It was so fucking great."

Ocasek persuaded the band to travel to his home base in Manhattan and record at Electric Lady Studios. Sharp and Cuomo had come up with all sorts of rules – they banned the use of reverb, for instance, and insisted on all downstrokes on guitar. "There was one overriding concept," says the album's engineer, Chris Shaw. "The idea that the guitars and the bass were one huge 10-string instrument. There's very few songs on the record to actually have a bass line that drifts away from what the guitar is doing." When they mixed the album, they insisted that all of the guitars be as loud as or louder than the ones on Radiohead's "Creep," which is why some of the vocals are almost buried.

Cuomo had written a song called "Buddy Holly," using a friend's Korg keyboard to add Eighties-ish synth parts. In his mind, it was intended for the band's second album, which would be more keyboard-oriented and New Wave-influenced. (Weezer, of course, never made such an album; Matt Sharp, destined to part ways with the group circa 1997, did instead, with his band the Rentals.) Sharp and Cuomo were also concerned that "Buddy Holly" could become the kind of Nineties hit that could kill a band. "There was a worry that it could become the 'Detachable Penis' of this album," says Sharp. "We had the sense that it could be taken as a novelty song, and people aren't going to take the album seriously." Ocasek lobbied hard for them to record it, even making a sign to request it during preproduction. It certainly was an obvious hit; during mixing, Shaw remembers stepping out of the control room to hear a receptionist humming it to herself.

Just before they finished recording, Weezer fired Cropper, and Cuomo replaced all of his guitar parts. Cropper is still convinced that he was canned mostly because of his relationship with his then-girlfriend, now his former wife, who was unpopular with the bandmates. She was pregnant with a first child, and, defying Cuomo's no-girlfriends-while-we're-recording diktat, flew to New York to visit Cropper. He also thinks Sharp had it out for him, and perhaps was jealous that he'd written the guitar intro to "My Name Is Jonas." Sharp gently says none of that is true. "There was no single event that triggered us letting Jason go," he says. Instead, a series of "tiny infractions" led Sharp to believe that the band's overall chemistry was at risk. "Since it was my obligation to try and ensure our basic survival," Sharp says, "I shared these concerns with Rivers, and with our limited life experience, we did what we thought was right. Next thing you know, Luca Brasi was swimming with the fishes." Cuomo felt that if they were going to make a change, it had to be before they finished the first album and shot the album cover.

For Cropper, it was a tough road at times, though he eventually reconciled with Cuomo and told him he was grateful for all the years he got to spend with his family. People on the L.A. music scene could be shockingly callous; one booker casually said, "Gosh, I'm surprised you haven't killed yourself." Cropper, whose kids have grown up, is working on a solo project that will include songs about his Weezer experience – he also performed with Cuomo in 2018. "I'm not just an ex-member of the band," he says. "I'm a huge fan."

Weezer needed a replacement, fast, and settled on a great-looking guy they'd seen around L.A.; Sharp was pretty sure that Brian Bell could play, but he wasn't entirely positive. "All I had was a foggy image in my head," says Sharp, "that he had one of those slight frames that kind of resembled the long lineage of wafer-thin, anorexic, archetypal guitar gods that we all grew up on." They had him overdub some parts on their demo as a test, and a quick phone interview that included a quiz on his favorite *Star Wars* action figure (Hammerhead) went well. Bell was in.

Bell flew to New York just in time to squeeze in some background vocals on Weezer's debut. When he arrived at their hotel, he knocked on Cuomo's door and discovered that the frontman had grown a robust "cop mustache." "First thing is, you have to grow a mustache," Cuomo told him. "Because we're all going to have mustaches on the front cover."

"Are you sure?" Bell asked him. (Fortunately, Cuomo wasn't sure.)

Bell got word that he would be sharing a room with Wilson. "So I go to Pat's room," Bell recalls, "and Pat goes, 'Welcome to Weezer!' And he just pulls his pants down and moons me. And I'm like, 'What the hell have I stepped into?'"

IN CLASSIC NINETIES fashion, Cuomo almost immediately realized he hated being a rock star. Weezer were hesitant to do music videos, but got along with the young director Spike Jonze, the only guy to pitch a "Sweater Song" video without any images of a sweater. When they teamed up with him again for a "Buddy Holly" video, he came up with the "Happy Days" idea, and the inevitable happened.

"I seriously thought we were the next Nirvana," Cuomo admits. "And I thought the world was going to perceive us that way, like a superimportant, superpowerful, heartbreaking heavy rock band, and as serious artists. That's how I saw us." The first clue that the world would see it slightly differently came in a lunch with Sullivan, who praised the humor of some of Cuomo's lyrics, even using the words "comical band." "It was just like a gut punch," Cuomo says. "And that's when I started to realize the world wasn't going to see Weezer like I did and the world wasn't going to see the Blue Album like I did." "Sweater Song," in particular, was about Cuomo's "darkest thoughts, and it became clear everyone else who hears this song is going to think it's hilarious."

He didn't enjoy touring, in part because of an entirely self-imposed mandate to play the same set list in the same order nearly every night. During a tour break, he wrote a lovely ballad called "Long Time Sunshine" that strongly suggested he wanted to quit rock, enroll in college on the East Coast, and get married. He became obsessed with classical music, and began sending out applications to elite East Coast institutions. "He told me, 'I think I want to go to school and be a classical musician,'" says Bell. "I'm like, 'Hey, dude, are you OK?'" Cuomo started asking for a piano in every hotel room and sought out opera performances on the band's European tour.

Cuomo picked Harvard after he realized he didn't have enough formal music training for Juilliard, his first choice. No one in the band will admit to worrying that it was all over when Cuomo matriculated, but it was definitely unnerving. "He was disillusioned," says Wilson. "And we were like, 'What the fuck? Can we please keep doing this?'" (Ocasek, for one, wasn't surprised: "That sounds about right," he thought when he heard the news.)

In the end, Cuomo's bandmates were correct; Weezer's weird story was just beginning, school or not. In the fall of 1995, Cuomo enrolled at Harvard, strolling through the leafy campus, just as he had dreamed. No one bugged him; it was as if Weezer never happened. There were papers to write, piles of reading to do. Sitting in his studio, Cuomo grins and recalls the thought that came to mind no more than two or three weeks into his first semester: "I kind of want to go back," he told himself, "to being in a band." ℞

Last' 6 Word

Clive Davis

The legendary music exec on FDR, bisexuality, Whitney, and Aretha

Who are your heroes?
FDR. He overcame personal handicaps and adversity to become one of the great leaders of all time. I would also say Jackie Robinson. I was a huge Brooklyn Dodgers fan growing up – I used to live six blocks from Ebbets Field. Not only was [Robinson] a great

> *Davis is working on an upcoming album of Whitney Houston songs.*

ballplayer, but he emerged as a role model to become the first black [major league] ballplayer.

Of all the artists you worked with who are no longer with us, who do you miss the most?
Whitney. We had a very close relationship professionally from the time I found her in 1983. I would say the story of Whitney Houston has clearly not been told yet. She's had two documentaries, and I think each of them failed to show the other side of Whitney, the side of her talent, her heart, why she was loved by so many. Her battle with drugs must be told, and how it prematurely caused her death. By no means whitewash it. But do not ignore the music and her natural talent, how she became the greatest singer of her generation.

Among the artists you've signed, whose records do you listen to the most?
The artist I probably play the most is Springsteen. And that includes the brand-new album – "There Goes My Miracle," "Tucson Train." I had nothing to do with it creatively. But I do love all of Springsteen. From being there at his signing to seeing him on Broadway, I've seen him over a lifetime.

When did you last speak with Aretha?
She and I became great friends. We would get together for dinner and talk about life. She never admitted she was terminally ill. We talked until a few weeks before she passed. She wanted every little detail of when I went to Saint-Tropez or St. Barts. She was always ready to overcome her fear of flying.

Which artist do you most regret not signing?
I was at dinner in 2004 with Bruce Springsteen, John Mellencamp, Jackson Browne, and Don Henley. I looked at Mellencamp and said, "It's so ironic that you're sitting next to Bruce, because I always picked you as the artist I most regretted not having signed. You were too close to Bruce at the time." And he said, "You were right. My biggest influence at the time was Bruce, and there's no question I was not ready to emerge as John Cougar to become the creative person I was. So I'm grateful to you."

What was your most self-indulgent purchase?
I rented a yacht for a number of years. The first time was probably about 20 years ago, for two weeks to parts of Capri and the French Riviera. It was a wonderful thrill, but it cost between $150,000 and $200,000 a week. My hands were shaking as I was signing the contract because it was clearly an indulgence.

What's the best advice you ever received?
Because I loved to read, my mother always told me never to live in an ivory tower and that it's vital to get out there and mix with people. She always would say, "You're not gonna get common sense from books, you're gonna get common sense from life and people." And she's right.

You came out as bisexual in your memoir six years ago. How do you look back at that moment?
I don't look upon it as the signal event in my life, but there was no way I was going to do an autobiography and not include the fact that only in middle age, after two failed marriages, would I look beyond gender for a relationship. I embraced bisexuality, which is the most misunderstood term in sexual identity.

I never felt it was understood by much of the straight or gay community. You had to be either gay or straight – there was no in between. I just opened myself up to the person rather than to the gender. I've read how, as some in the younger generation try to find their sexual identity, it doesn't make any difference which gender it is until they locate the person. I relate to that. DAVID BROWNE